# IN-WORDS & OUT-WORDS

*By the same author*
The Joy of Words

# FRITZ SPIEGL'S
## IN-WORDS & OUT-WORDS

### A Browser's Guide to

Archaisms ... Euphemisms ... Colloquialisms
Genteelisms ... Neologisms ... Americanisms
Loony Leftisms ... Solecisms ... Idiotisms

### With a Colour Supplement

ELM TREE BOOKS · LONDON

ELM TREE BOOKS

Penguin Books Ltd, 27 Wrights Lane, London W8 5TZ (Publishing &
Editorial)
*and* Harmondsworth, Middlesex, England (Distribution & Warehouse)
Viking Penguin Inc., 40 West 23rd Street, New York, New York 10010,
U.S.A.
Penguin Books Australia Ltd, Ringwood, Victoria, Australia
Penguin Books Canada Limited, 2801 John Street, Markham, Ontario,
Canada L3R 1B4
Penguin Books (N.Z.) Ltd, 182–190 Wairau Road, Auckland 10, New
Zealand

First published in Great Britain 1987 by
Elm Tree Books

British Library Cataloguing-in-Publication Data:

Spiegl, Fritz
  In-words & out-words
  1. English language Usage
  I. Title
  428.1    PE1460

ISBN 0–241–12430–1
ISBN 0–241–12429–8 pbk

Typeset in $9\frac{1}{2}/11\frac{1}{2}$ pt Rockwell by
Butler & Tanner.
Printed and bound in Great Britain
by Butler & Tanner, Frome, Somerset

for D.A.S.

# FORWARD*

This is not a dictionary but an alphabetical browsing-book. It is intended for the person who takes notice of the words we use, or the way they are used by those who have something to hide, to sell, or some unpalatable facts to disguise; and these MINI-essays on In-words and Out-words (small capitals denote cross-references throughout) are meant for the person who is not easily deceived, who does not blindly follow the latest fad or fashion – in everyday speech or anything else. He also likes to find out *why* his vocabulary is changing; and to pursue the sources and origins of words both old and new. When he consults a dictionary he usually gets diverted beyond his immediate purpose and delights in finding words he did not seek. Which, I hope, is what will happen when he opens this book, although some of the cross-references will send the reader on a circular route back to where he started.

The reader I have in mind probably also deplores wilful changes in the meaning of beautiful English words, yet he does not cling pedantically to archaisms. Many words get thrown up by events, politics, the WELFARE STATE, wars and conflicts (like YOMPING, which came in during the Falklands war, and went out again); other words shift their ground, or are annexed by certain groups. Many Americanisms – imaginative inventions, usually, though seldom beautiful – that were once derided are now indispensable, like the ubiquitous COMMUTER. American words like SCIENTIST were reviled in England during the 19th century, but the protesters soon gave up, because people liked the word and took to it. Another Americanism, FRUITIST, also dating from the last century, disappeared again. And a century before the STRIPPAGRAM came into fashion, America had the Happygram. Although this is not an account of the differences between British and American English, I have included various PENTAGONISMS and HAIGISMS which

* A friend, a professor at an English university, opened a doctoral thesis he was assessing and was confronted by the word 'Forward' heading the student's introduction. He pencilled underneath it the annotation, 'Let's hope so!'

American politicians and spokesmen appear to find necessary for disguising unpleasant truths.

In addition, my ideal reader will be one who, if he sees a DEMO will probably walk in the other direction rather than join it, let alone shout SLOGANS (a word with a delightfully apt history). He will be politically a little cynical, not committed (see COMMITMENT) to a particular dogma or *ism,* for he has heard all the clichés before. And, if a woman, my reader will be sensible enough not to be offended by the word 'he', for those who are not WIMMIN bitten by the extremist bug know that in language, 'man embraces woman'; and besides, that life is too short to keep saying 'he or she', let alone resort to false plurals, foolish inventions like 'shim', or address someone who is obviously human as a CHAIR. My ideal reader will read REAL newspapers, BROADSHEETS like the *Times,* the *Daily Telegraph,* the *Guardian* or the *Independent,* and not be taken in by the sensational, language-mangling TABLOIDS, though he may wince at their repetitive, punning language.

Another reason for disclaiming the status of a dictionary for this book is that dictionaries are supposed to be objective and dispassionate. This one makes judgments on almost every page, and some are sure to be challenged.

Many *isms* and their *ists* have over the years changed sides. The Chartists and early SOCIALists were fiercely proud of theirs, which simply described the causes they passionately believed in. Russian czars ruled by terrorising their subjects – and were therefore described in the free world as TERRORISTS – a word which has changed its connotations. Those who advocated revolution – in German, a *Putsch* – against the czars' despotism were, for a time, called PUTSCHists. Women who, quite rightly, wish to abolish discrimination against their sex, are feminists. Like CONSUMERists they occupy the old ground. Yet they describe those who do discriminate *against* them as sexist. The self-satirising LOONY local authorities have shown themselves to be tireless inventors of *isms* of the second sort, their own particular pet words with which to describe actions they believe are to be deplored, as indeed most of them were by right-thinking people long before these loonies came to power. But they now invent silly names like ageism, 'discrimination against the old', and ableism, meaning 'discrimination in favour of the able-bodied'. And as this book goes to press, Haringey Council in London is appointing an £11,000-a-year Animal Rights Officer whose brief is to fight speciesism, 'discrimination by humans against another animal because it is of a different species'.

These are aberrations which may not do much for the beauty of the language but they help to keep English alive and make it even more accessible to an ever-growing number of people. When Samuel Daniel in 1599 wrote his *Musophilus* (translatable as 'Lover of Sounds' – in this context meaning the beautiful sound of English), he cleverly foresaw that our (yes, *our*) language would go out from this tiny island to become the most widely-understood means of communication in the world:

> *And who in time knows whither we may vent*
> *The treasure of our tongue? To what strange shores*
> *This gain of our best glory shall be sent,*
> *T'enrich unknowing nations with our stores?*
> *What worlds in th' yet unformed Occident*
> *May come refin'd with the accents that are ours?*

I have also included a number of catch-phrases which have achieved cliché status, words that have changed their meanings, or simply words that took my fancy or had interesting origins, or which just happened to be the result of research into other words.

The use of colours in everyday speech – either factual or figurative – is so wide that I have included a Colour Supplement. Cross-references may refer both to the Supplement and the main body of the book. *Isms* plays a big part in this book, and most of them seem to be political. A radio listener sent me a set of definitions which he had long had in his possession but was unable to attribute to an author. I quote it with acknowledgment.

SOCIALISM: You have two cows. You give one to your neighbour.
COMMUNISM: You have two cows. The government takes them both and gives you a little milk.
TRADE UNIONISM: You have two cows. The union takes both from you, shoots one, milks the other – and throws the milk away.
FASCISM: You have two cows. The government takes both and shoots you.
NAZISM: You have two cows. You sell them both and buy a bull.

However, I prefer the definition of communism given in Russia over the non-existent subversive Radio Armenia 'Radio Erivan' (surely a reference to Samuel Butler's *Erewhon* – i.e. 'nowhere' spelt backwards). Capitalism is the oppression and exploitation of man by man. Communism? The other way round.

# A

**Abattoir** The Englishman's love and care for animals is known throughout the world and derided by some, although it is one of the distinguishing marks of a civilised people. Perhaps that is why he prefers to use the French word for a slaughterhouse, a GENTEELISM if there ever was one, intended perhaps to ease the conscience. But abattoir comes from *abattre*, to batter, beat down, destroy, do away with. (See BATTERED WIVES.) But see also EURO- for the old theory of why French words are preferred for food; and STOP, which is a sporting euphemism for knocking someone senseless in a boxing-ring.

**Ableism** Described by 'Peterborough' in the *Daily Telegraph* who spotted it in a press release from Haringey Council as 'the ism to cap the lot'. It means 'discrimination in favour of the able-bodied when engaging workers for building-sites, etc.', and is a worthy addition to the growing number of increasingly weird coinages emanating from LOONY local authorities.

**Ablutions** GENTEELISM for washing, usually only one's hands or face, and often used with studied facetiousness. However, the wash-rooms near the Reading-room of the British Museum (now needlessly renamed the British Library) display a notice warning visitors that 'These Basins are for Casual Ablutions Only', thus prohibiting major 'detergings' – for the modern soap-substitutes are named after the Latin *de+ tergere*, to wipe off. See also WASHING HANDS.

**Abo** See JAP.

**Abort** Until the advent of space travel this was an ominous sort of word, with dark undertones of illegal abortions (from L. *abortus*, an untimely birth). But it has also been used figuratively, of something unsuccessful in attaining its desired end or effect, since Shakespeare: 'Let it make thee Crest-falne, I, and alaye this thy abortiue Pride' (*Henry VI Part 2*). Today, however, small children acting out space games and fantasies can be seen and heard running round their playgrounds crying, 'Abort! Abort!' See also TERMINATION.

**Abrasive**  Euphemism for rude, especially when said of a public figure.

**Absolutely**  An emphatic 'yes'.

**Access**  Vogue prefix, e.g. 'Access Television', or 'Access Newspaper', indicating the temporary throwing-open of communications media to ordinary people. Access Television offers a few minutes' air-time, which makes little difference to those getting 'access', but makes the monopoly-holder feel a little better. There is a whole corpus of applications, e.g. the alleged 'accessibility' of officials and politicians, which in practice is largely a sham.

**Acronym**  Making silly new words by taking parts of old ones and stringing them together. No examples are necessary, as modern life is full of them. But although the craze has probably only now reached its peak, it was begun long ago, in Soviet Russia (with, even, some earlier examples dating from Czarist times), and copied with a vengeance in Nazi Germany, for the practice lends itself admirably to the temporary disguise of unpleasant truths. See also AIDS, below.

**-Action**  Media, political and commercial cliché, when combined with a prefix element, e.g. Cleansing Action, COMMUNITY Action; and often means inaction, as in the general euphemism for striking, 'Industrial Action'.

**Adult**  When used adjectivally this now often means 'juvenile, immature', as in adult films, books, videos, etc. See also EXPLICIT.

**Aerobics**  Short for aerobic exercises. This craze (like jogging) started in the United States during the 1980s and has acquired a certain vogue in Britain. The name echoes Jacques-Dalcroze's Eurhythmics, described in 1912 as 'the new craze, rhythmic exercises to music'. Aerobics is violent and strenuous exercising to loud and violent pop music (nearly always by women keen to improve their figure). Long or short, the term is absurd. 'Aerobic' comes from the Greek words for air + life. An anaerobic environment is one that has no oxygen and no life. It would be interesting to see someone doing *an*aerobic exercises.

**Affirmative** In American, a GENTEELISM for 'yes', and an abbreviation of the HAIGISM 'The answer is in the affirmative' – which was presumably considered more affirmative than a plain and easily missed 'yes'.

**Afro-saxon** A Negro whom others of the black race consider too willing to conform to white society and/or to adopt the prevailing white customs and life-style. See also OREO, UNCLE TOMISM and WASP.

**Agonising reappraisal** A once modish term for self-critical reassessment. It is included here as an example of how cliché fashions change. The term was first used by the American politician John Foster Dulles in 1953 and was soon on the lips of all politicians and businessmen eager to show how self-aware they were; but the novelty has long since worn off and the expression is now seldom heard except satirically.

**-Aid** Vogue suffix of 1985/6 and subsequently. From Band Aid, which was the fund-raising idea of a pop entertainer, Bob Geldof, Hon. KBE. He collected together a group of colleagues to make a record of pop music for world-wide sale in aid of starving people of Africa. This started a beneficent trend and before long there was Live Aid, Classics Aid, Aids Aid, Water Aid and even Drugs Aid (which is ironical, as many of the participating pop performers in the Band Aid venture were either active, convicted, or reformed drugs misusers and in danger of contracting AIDS). The original Band Aid was a punning reference to the trade-name of a medicated first-aid plaster which is still being sold and whose shareholders must have been delighted by the free advertising.

**Aids** A loosely-constructed ACRONYM for the deadly Acquired Immunodeficiency Syndrome. This is its scientific name; *not*, as even the most respected journalists have decided, Acquired *Immune Deficiency* Syndrome (see also SYNDROME); for this nonsensically means that it is the deficiency which is immune. But as commonly happens with such verbal annexations, the hijackers get away with murder, and thus even the *British Medical Journal* has bowed to 'Immune Deficiency' (while its sister-paper, *The Lancet*, commendably insists on the correct form). Here, too (as with -AID, above), there is a commercial product with a soundalike name, a slimming-aid called AYDS, which is having a

hard time. The disease was first recognised in Africa, where it is
called 'Slim' because people afflicted with it there waste away,
and has been called the 'Green Monkey Disease' because it was
thought to have been carried by the animals and was at first
restricted to Africans and monkeys, and later to promiscuous
American homosexuals (the 'Gay Plague') and drug-abusers. But
it was soon realised that it could be spread via infected blood to
haemophiliacs, women, their babies and to heterosexual men. Its
dangers were widely publicised in Britain (though most other
countries ignored the dangers and some, e.g. in Africa, actively
suppressed them so as not to discourage tourists). The most
widespread publicity campaign ever attempted was mounted in
Britain in 1986/7, with 95-year-old pensioners and pre-pubescent
schoolchildren alike receiving relentless exhortations by
television and house-to-house LEAFLETTING always to use a CONDOM
when engaging in anal intercourse. Some cynics said it was an
over-reaction to make the government appear to be a CARING one,
others that the publicity should have been aimed more specifically
at homosexuals and drugs-abusers (by that time only four women
had been infected, and a minuscule number of heterosexual men),
or similar efforts made to combat the many thousands each year
who died needlessly from heart disease and road accidents. Anti-
Americans immediately claimed that the virus was man-made by
politically-motivated scientists and had 'escaped' from their –
doubtless CIA-funded – laboratories. Only time will tell whether
AIDS is 'the greatest threat to human life since the Black Death'.

**Air support** Euphemism of the United States Army and CIA
(Central Intelligence Agency) for bombing, originating from the
Korean War but best remembered from Vietnam use: one of
several PENTAGONISMS described in these pages, e.g. NATURAL
RESURFACE CONTROL PROGRAMME, etc. Contrary to allegations, 'Air
support' is not a euphemism for the bombing of civilians, but for
any kind of bombardment – more an example of HAIGSPEAK. When
civilians were bombed, either by accident or design, it was called
'incontinent ordinance'.

**Album** In popular (and increasingly also 'classical') musical
jargon, a full-sized gramophone record which is not a 78 or a
single or a compact disc.

**Alcohol abuse** Euphemism for drunkenness, one of many devised by CARING sociologists, who would, for example, describe a drunken tramp as an 'alcohol dependent vagrant'. See also DRUG ABUSE.

**Alibi** Latin for 'elsewhere'; not for an excuse, as is often supposed.

**Alley** Suffix preceded by a facetious description of a certain place, e.g. Bomb Alley, Tarts Alley, etc. See also -VILLE.

**Alternative** A fashionable prefix word of the 1950s and subsequently, and often used as a kind of trendy alternative to 'alternate' on the mistaken principle that words that end with -ive are somehow more impressive than those that do not. Alternate, from Latin *alternare*, means 'every second', i.e. in alternation, as in 'Meetings are held on alternate Tuesdays'. Alternative means 'one *or* the other', and 'Meetings held on alternative Tuesdays' (often seen and heard) is nonsense. The Alternative Society, that great refuge of DROP-OUTS and beat-NIKS, started the trend, and meant a style of life followed by persons with a less conventional outlook. Newspapers gave them column-inches under titles like 'The Alternative Voice', FOODIES of various kinds, including vegetarians, vegans and others with strong views, demanded alternative eating, hippies and PUNKS sport an alternative hairstyle, perhaps ride bicycles as alternative transport – and in fact the whole thing has got out of hand. People who wish to be rehoused invariably ask for 'alternative accommodation'.

**-ama** Vogue ending in commerce and entertainment, probably starting with the American cinerama and leading to shopperama, launderama, stripperama, etc. Shops and stores are also constantly searching for ever more impressive size prefixes, like super-, hyper-, and now MEGA-.

**Amanuensis** A much-neglected word for a secretary, a helper, or one who writes to another's dictation. From *a manu* (short for *servus a manu*) + *ensis*, the suffix which indicates the state of belonging. A good word, therefore, for someone who waits 'hand and foot'. An amanuensis is usually thought to be male, but the female would be a handmaiden. See GIRL FRIDAY.

**Ambassador**  See DIPLOMAT.

**Angst**  In German this is the ordinary, everyday word for fear. Children who are afraid of the dark, an examination, the bogeyman (or whatever) say, *Ich habe Angst*. In English, however, *angst* (with a small a) 'denotes a certain condition as of expectation of danger ... even though it may be an unknown one'. That is how C. J. M. Hubback explained it in his translation of the works of Sigmund Freud, leaving it untranslated instead of simply using the English word 'anxiety', which would have done perfectly well, for that is what it means.

**Announcement**  Disc-jockeys' euphemism on COMMERCIAL radio for a 'commercial', i.e. a paid-for advertisement. Calling it an announcement is more likely to persuade the listener to take notice. As, 'We'll be right back after this announcement'. See also BREAK and DEDICATION, as well as MESSAGE.

**A. N. Other**  See WALTER PLINGE.

**-Artist**  Sarcastic suffix applied to someone allegedly possessing certain qualities that are never related to art and are usually of a NEGATIVE nature, .e.g. piss artist (a heavy drinker), shortchange artist, hot air artist (who talks a lot), etc.

**Aspirations**  A more recently-fashionable synonym for demands or ambitions, epecially in negotiations for higher wages and a favourite of trades union officials, e.g. 'my members' legitimate aspirations ...'. In its Latin form it literally means 'sighing towards or for' some desired object.

**As told to ...**  The formula used in books or newspaper articles to indicate that the real work was done by a GHOST.

**Astronomical**  In the debased language of political and trades union jargon this has nothing to do with the stars but merely means a lot of money, as in 'astronomical price rises'. But even it is subject to further corruption, as when a shop steward claimed that Fords were 'paying wages astronomically lower than anyone else'.

**-(a)thon**  See MARATHON.

**-ation**  Many words with this often superfluous ending are adaptations by the Americans from the German in which many of them (or their ancestors) were brought up, e.g. transport(ation), transplant(ation) etc. Sometimes suffix is piled upon suffix, as in 'hospitalisation', meaning the state of being in, or going into, hospital.

**At this (point/moment in) time**  American-based term of German origin (*Zu diesem Zeitpunkt*) meaning 'now'. Also 'currently', 'at this juncture', 'presently', etc. Like many HAIGISMS it can be extended, e.g. 'At this very present and particular moment in time ...'.

**Awareness**  A quality said to be necessary for modern men and women to possess, and not only if they belong to a minority group. To be 'aware' one merely has to be – well – aware, usually without specification of what or whom one is aware of. This is not unrelated to the equally loosely-defined state of CONSCIOUSNESS. In November 1986 the Department of Trade and Industry instigated what was described as 'an Awareness Programme' for the UNWAGED.

**Awful**  A prime example of the way in which the meaning of words can be both changed and rendered less effective. In the middle ages, from around 800 A.D., its meaning was nearer to (but stronger than) the present one – terrible, dreadful, appalling (which has suffered a loss in meaning in much the same manner). From about 1000 A.D., God and His self-appointed representatives, the kings and princes, were described as awful – solemnly majestic, sublimely impressive – that is, inspiring awe in their subjects and proud of it. Hence Shakespeare's use, often in the sense of respectful or reverential. In the early 19th century the Americans started to batter the word into an awful submission, and by 1834 Charles Lamb used it about an ugly, unpleasant woman, while qualifying it with a nod across the Atlantic: 'She is indeed, as the Americans would express it, something awful'. By the late Victorian era, 'awf'ly' – meaning anything from 'very' to

**THE SLANG OF THE DAY.**

*(Fragment of Fashionable Conversation.)*

*Youth.* "A—AWFUL HOT, AIN'T IT?"
*Maiden.* "YES, AWFUL!" *(Pause.)*
*Youth.* "A—AWFUL JOLLY FLOOR FOR DANCING, AIN'T IT?"
*Maiden.* "YES, AWFUL!" *(Pause.)*
*Youth.* "A—A—AWFUL JOLLY SAD ABOUT THE POOR DUCHESS, AIN'T IT?"
*Maiden.* "YES—QUITE TOO AWFUL——" *(And so forth.)*

*Punch, 5th August 1871*

'slightly' – had arrived; and still reigns supreme, in spite of the even greater debasement of BLOODY.

**Aztec two-step** Travellers' diarrhoea, the traditional affliction suffered by visitors to Mexico, where it is also known as Montezuma's Revenge. The Mexicans themselves call the affliction *turista*. Also Delhi Belly, Basra Belly, Bombay Crud and Hong Kong Dog, etc., according to location.

# B

**Backlash**  A strong reaction, often over-reaction: the white backlash, black backlash, student backlash, etc. In fashionable use in the USA from the 1960s, and well defined as 'the bigotry of the majority'. The Americans have also coined a backlash word to backlash, which is 'frontlash', and means a desirable and laudable under-reaction to an over-reaction.

**Backroom boys**  Scientists. See also BOFFINS.

**Backward**  As in 'backward nations'. See EMERGENT.

**Balkanisation**  Some people speak of 'the balkanisation of British industry': a strangely dated term which (says the 1972 Supplement to the Oxford English Dictionary) means splitting something into many small and competing parts, as was done to countries of the Balkan peninsula during the late 19th and early 20th century with disastrous results – but without in the least deterring present-day would-be balkanising SEPARATISTS.

**Ballgame**  Not a game, or not necessarily a game involving a ball or balls, but an American-based cliché for the matter in hand, the business under consideration, the current project or situation. As in 'That's a different ballgame altogether ...'. When the boxer Cassius Clay ('Muhammad Ali') met his final defeat in October 1980 his manager Angelo Dundee entered the ring and declared, 'The ballgame is over'.

**Ballpark figure** In American business jargon, and occasionally heard from British TYCOONS who wish to present an image of American dynamism, this means an approximate figure or sum of money.

**Banana(s)** This tropical fruit became familiar in Europe only comparatively recently, and cheap enough to be available to ordinary people only during the 1920s and early 30s, after the spread of refrigerated shipping. But the British soon took a fancy to the fruit, immortalising it both in comic songs and lewd allusions, which appealed to song-writers: *I had a Banana with Lady Diana* was a thinly-disguised allusion to Lady Diana Cooper (née Manners) and her allegedly prolific sex-life ('having a banana' with someone was the same kind of euphemism as UGANDAN DISCUSSIONS are now); and *Yes, we have no Bananas* (1923) may have owed at least part of its popularity to the fact that the authors (Silver and Cohn) stole the first four notes of the tune from Handel's *Hallelujah* Chorus. A *Serenade* by D. G. D. Ainslie, quoted in Ivor Brown's *Chosen Words* (Cape, 1955) has the lines *Lady of the lovely thighs/Curving like banana fruit*; and the five-note chorus phrase *'Have a banana!'* was always guaranteed to raise a lewd laugh in the music-halls. 'Going bananas' is one of many jocular synonyms for alleged madness, perhaps an allusion to its bent shape (*cf* 'going round the bend'). Banana Republics are small countries in Africa or South America whose economy is almost entirely based on the export of bananas, and who suffer (as most South American and African states do) from an unstable, despotic and cruel regime. Ralph Waldo Emerson wrote perceptively and prophetically (though forgetting the Russian czars and not yet knowing what their successors would be like):

> The highest civility has never loved the hot zones.
> Where snow falls there is usually civil freedom;
> Where the banana grows, man is sensual and cruel.

Of more recent usage, invented by JOURNOS and HACKS in descriptions of THATCHERISM, are the political banana-skins, meaning slip-ups, something like an OWN GOAL in the PROPAGANDA war of politics. After several such episodes the British Government was said to have appointed what the popular press dubbed a 'Minister for Banana Skins'. The word, which is Hispanic in origin, appeals because of its comic reduplication. Originally only the fruit was a *banana*, and the tree on which it grows, a *banano*. The Congolese name is *Pigafetta*, but it is perhaps worth adding that the first president of the People's Republic of Zimbabwe (formerly Rhodesia) was a Mr Banana, and that one of the first encroachments on free speech in that banana republic was the banning of jokes on his name. Nevertheless, when the president had a political disagreement with his colleagues, the propaganda ministry denied there had 'been any split between President Banana and Mr Mugabe'. Some Bible scholars have recently suggested (perhaps not too seriously) that in the Adam and Eve legend the Tree of Knowledge was not an apple-tree but bore bananas; and that the first couple covered their nakedness more effectively in banana rather than fig-leaves.

**Bandwagons**  These always 'roll' or are 'mounted'; and, in their political sense, stem from the use politicians and political candidates have always made of the power of music to collect a crowd and induce sympathetic or rousing feelings in uncommitted bystanders. Originally from circus usage, when the band would travel on a separate wagon (and led the circus procession into town by the longest route possible, by way of advertising its presence and drumming up custom). The first political bandwagon is thought to have rolled in 1884, carrying an American presidential candidate and his supporters.

**Bang**  One of those convenient English colloquialisms which can be applied to many concepts and things. The de-regulation of the Stock Exchange in October 1986 became known (and was always referred to without further explanation) as the Big Bang. It was a momentous event in the history of this ancient and convention-bound institution. The term immediately suggests the Big Bang Theory, a disputed view about the way in which the universe was created, from which the 'big' was probably borrowed for reasons of euphony and alliteration. But 'to bang' has since Victorian days been part of financial jargon and meant, even in the 1880s, 'Loudly or recklessly to offer stock on the open market, with the intention of lowering the price if necessary'. To be 'bang on' means to be accurate; but to 'bang on' ('and on and on and on') is to talk too much about a specific – and uninteresting – subject. A printer or other newspaper worker who retires is noisily 'banged out' by his colleagues with type-sticks and other printers' furniture of the old technology. There is also the sexual connotation: the same as 'knocking', 'knocking-shop' etc., which like the more common rude word (which comes from an old Germanic word *fikken*, to strike hard) suggests a crude, violent and primitive approach to the sexual act. The expression 'Bang went sixpence' comes from a *Punch* cartoon of 5th December 1868 which (like GOOD IN PARTS) has acquired the status of a cliché-proverb.

**Banger**  Not one who bangs but, most commonly, an English sausage. Also the nickname for a shabby old car in questionable running-order but not old enough to qualify for the description of 'veteran' (usually pre-1911 though sometimes applied to any car over 50 years old) or 'vintage' (pre-1930). For cherished and well-kept cars of a later period, e.g. the 1950s, 'thoroughbred' is borrowed from horse-racing parlance.

**Barbecue**  Open-air cookery (or the apparatus used for it) which American Indians resorted to because they lacked appliances for preparing their food in a more convenient manner. But modern American man decided he liked occasionally to revert to the primitive, picturesque ways (just as animal hides were worn by primitive man because they were more easily available than fabrics and then became the fashion again in modern times). Hence the vogue for the barbecue, which has spread worldwide, especially to British suburban patios. The OED has a reference quoting a traveller in the colony of Virginia, who wrote in 1705 that the Indians 'have two ways of Broyling, viz. one by laying the Meat upon Sticks rais'd upon Forks at some distance above the live Coals . . . this they, and we also from them, call Barbacueing'. Frenchmen would probably prefer to point to a Parisian slang word for meat, *barbaque*; and Rumanians (who, like all Balkan people, roast meat on skewers over an open fire) would say that they have a word, *barbec*, meaning meat. And South American Spanish-speaking people (some of whom by 1705 would have mixed with Virginian Indians and lent them a word or two) have a contraption called *barbacoa*, which is a raised, meshed, mattress-like platform which could be used for lying upon (e.g. for a siesta) or for cooking when a fire was made beneath it. Many Americans now prefer the simpler word cookout (see -OUT), perhaps in order to distinguish the noun from the adjectival barbecue which, in JUNK-food sales jargon, is intended to suggest that the product in question has a slightly sour and spicy taste, e.g. 'Bar-b-q Flavoured Prawn Crisps'.

**Basra belly**  See AZTEC TWO-STEP.

**Battered wives**  Women allegedly ill-treated by their husbands, a news-term chosen for its alliteratively dramatic ring. Physical abuse is suggested but it does not necessarily extend to the kind of battering the animals receive in the ABATTOIR. There are also battered babies, battered husbands and even battered grannies. People are declared to be battered if they are found to have what the social-workers euphemise as 'non-accidental injuries'.

**Because it is (was) there**  A reason said to have been given by Sir Edmund Hillary when he was asked why he had climbed Everest; but Hillary was quoting the earlier mountaineer George Leigh Mallory (1886–1924) who said it first. Although the phrase has become a cliché, people are nowadays more likely to give it as an excuse for embarking on a foolhardy or dangerous enterprise ('it's the challenge'). According to a letter in the *Daily Telegraph* (11 November 1986) from Mallory's niece, Mrs B. M. Newton Dunn, the mountaineer gave that reply to his sister (her mother) out of impatience, 'because a silly question deserves a silly answer'.

**Better red than dead**  The idea that it is better to be alive under COMMUNISM than dead but enjoying freedom was first propounded (only rather more elegantly) by the philosopher and pacifist Bertrand, third Earl Russell (1872–1970) in 1958, and 'SLOGANised' by the press a little later.

**Between jobs**  Euphemism for unemployed. See also CONSULTANCY and REDUNDANT.

**Blackmail**  This word has an interesting history, and no connection with letters of extortion received by mail. Long before there was a Penny Post or any other kind of organised postal system the word 'mail' denoted a tribute, or a payment of rent. It is an adaptation (by a bad speller?) from the Old Norse word

*mali*, a stipulation, or agreed pay. Blackmail was a product of the
Anglo-Scottish border lawlessness and feuding: 'a tribute
formerly exacted from farmers and small owners in the border
counties of England and Scotland, and along the Highland border,
by freebooting chiefs, in return for protection or immunity from
plunder'. In other words, a forerunner of the PROTECTION racket
still run by the 'freebooting chiefs' on both sides of the conflict in
Northern Ireland. See the Colour Supplement for some of the
wider uses of BLACK.

**Blitz**  A relic of the Second World War, being an abbreviation of
the German *Blitzkrieg*, or lightning-war, which is what Hitler
threatened to inflict on Europe from 1938. By this he meant that
with the help of his supposedly superior air-power and panzer
forces he would over-run his enemies with lightning speed. To
English ears the word had a ridiculous sound (as did Hitler's silly,
high-pitched and hysterical voice), and *Blitz* was first turned
against the German enemy and then adopted as an English verbal
trophy of war. It is now perfectly at home in the language ('I must
have a blitz on all my unanswered letters . . .') as a naturalised
English word and without the initial capital it takes in German.

**Blockbuster**  During the BLITZ, the popular name for a kind of
huge aerial bomb dropped by the Germans on English cities,
often by parachute, when they were also called parachute mines.
They caused enormous damage, often destroying whole blocks
of houses. In America, where no German bombs fell (and where,
incidentally, to be blitzed means to be drunk) blockbusting after
the Second World War acquired a different meaning, 'to persuade
white property owners to sell their homes quickly and often below
true value for fear that Negroes will move into the area', and a
blockbuster is 'a real-estate agent who practises blockbusting'
(Wentworth & Flexner: *Dictionary of American Slang*). But since
the 1970s the meaning most commonly understood is of a very
successful – and almost always trashy – book, or sometimes a film
with great box-office appeal. Such blockbusters are bound as
paperbacks, making up in bulk and weight what they lack in
literary quality and intellectual substance, and are often PACKAGED
or perhaps even largely the work of a GHOST or ghosts.

**Bloody** Much has been written about this word and its alleged – but doubtful – origin as an early English Catholic oath 'By our Lady!' (although, of course, it always retained its primary meaning relating to blood or bloodshed). The first edition of the OED supposed it to be a reference to a gang of notorious aristocratic rowdies during the late 17th and early 18th centuries, who would now be called HOORAY HENRYS. They were colloquially known as 'the bloods', and expressions like 'bloody behaviour' or 'bloody drunk' meant behaving like a blood or being drunk as a blood (compare with 'drunk as a lord' – see MLUD). One of them, Sir Charles Sedley, is reported by Samuel Pepys for 'baring his arse' in the street (see MOONING). Thus bloody became 'an intensification of "very", and was 'in general colloquial use until ca. 1750; now constantly in the mouths of the lowest classes but by respectable people considered "a horrid word", on a par with obscene or profane language, and printed in the newspapers (in police reports etc.,) as "b - - - y" '. Things have come a long way since then, and there is little in the way of OBSCENE words the newspapers refrain from printing. And euphemisms like 'Not Pygmalion likely' (from George Bernard Shaw's coyly daring use of 'bloody' in the play of that name in 1912), 'blooming', 'bleeding' or 'blessed' are considered unnecessary, at least by those who have moved on to stronger expletives.

**Boffin** At first this was Royal Navy slang for an elderly officer, but later (and now almost exclusively) meaning a BACKROOM BOY, that is, a scientist engaged in important and probably secret work. In this sense the word was popularised and established in informal English usage by Nevil Shute (1899–1960) after he used it in his novel *No Highway* (1948).

**Bolshy** Russian Bolsheviks were members of the Leninist faction that emerged triumphant after the October 1917 revolution which resulted from one of the splits that have now become traditional in extremist politics. Bolsheviks (in England 'Bolshevist' was for a time in parallel use) comes from the Russian word *bolshoi*, meaning large or big (so the Bolshoi is the Russian equivalent of the Grand Theatre!). Hence, in figurative colloquial usage, the adjective bolshy, applied to anyone considered recalcitrant or perhaps spitefully unhelpful. Trades union leaders are often so described (in private) by industrialists, but do not have to have any particular political allegiance to be bolshy. See also REVISIONISM and other cross-references concerning different aspects of disagreement with the Soviet SYSTEM.

**Bombay crud**  See AZTEC TWO-STEP and the various cross-references.

**Born-again**  As in 'born-again Christian': an indication of alleged spiritual rebirth, or a conversion so powerful that the fortunate subject feels like a new person. At first only heard in the religious sense but now in widespread facetious use, e.g. 'He's a born-again socialist', said of someone who has – or says he has, for political expediency – renounced his allegiance to MILITANT.

**Bottle**  A slang word with opposing meanings: either fear, from Cockney rhyming-slang 'bottle of beer/fear' or as courage, as in 'he lost his bottle', i.e. his nerve.

**Bottoming out**  'The downturn is bottoming out,' said an American president when he meant that times were getting better. The expression comes from VISUAL AIDS which show trends by means of graphs. See also (A) SLICE OF THE CAKE.

**Boutique**  The ordinary French word for a shop, but in English a pretentious name for one. See also the -TIQUE ending, and its various cross-references.

**Brainwash**  To try to change radically a person's attitude by intensive persuasion, interrogation and other psychological or pseudo-educational means. Brainwashing sometimes also involves the use of drugs (see PSYCHIATRIC HOSPITAL). It is a communist invention and the coinage, which is American, dates from the Korean War.

**Brave new world**  From the title of a futuristic novel written in 1932 by Aldous Huxley; now a cliché.

**Bread**  American slang word current among hippies meaning money. It dates from the late 1950s and 60s, and was soon used by British CATS and chicks who thought it was REAL cool to do so, MAN.

During the late 1970s it fell into almost complete disuse. Wentworth & Flexner trace its origin to the 1930s, when it was used exclusively by Negro jazz musicians. A former member of the unwashed and UNWAGED confessed that he went into a shop to buy a loaf of bread when he suddenly remembered that he had forgotten to bring his money. Having asked for bread he told the girl shop-assistant, 'Sorry, man, but I haven't got any bread!' In 1982 a robber was convicted for an attempted armed hold-up in a London café owned by a Greek immigrant. The culprit was caught because he kept demanding, 'Give me some bread!' The Greek, frightened but at the same time puzzled, handed the man a sliced loaf, which he rejected. The resulting delay enabled the police to arrest him.

**Break** As in 'Winter Break', a euphemism for a holiday, perhaps for the purpose of RECHARGING ONE'S BATTERIES. Also, in COMMERCIAL radio and television jargon, an ANNOUNCEMENT or MESSAGE.

**Break a leg!** An American expression of good (!) wishes, much used in the theatrical and musical professions. It is a direct but slightly softened translation from the similarly-used German *'Hals-und Beinbruch!'* – 'May you break your neck and leg!' – which is based on the old superstition that an unpleasant event expected and foreseen is as good as averted if expressed as a facetious wish. Now associated with Jewish/American usage.

**Breaking the mould.** A phrase which now denotes welcome and overdue change from an old order. It was coined by the ex-Labour ex-minister Roy Jenkins when, as part of The Gang of Four, he founded the Social Democratic Party in 1981. What he intended to suggest was that British politics had for too long been cast in the old two-party mould, like some mass-produced artifact; and that thenceforth things would be new and different. It certainly seems that with the advent of the SDP/Liberal Alliance British politics will never be the same again. But Mr Jenkins in fact misapplied a term used by sculptors in a quite different context. To them, 'breaking the mould' after a piece of sculpture has been cast in bronze (or whatever) is a way of ensuring that a particular work of art is unique (or at least limited to an authorised number of casts). In other words, it is a safeguard for the buyer, who knows that his neighbour will not be able to display the same work in his own house. The same thing may apply to plates of an etching or engraving after numbered-and-signed copies have been made. The English translation of Ariosto's *Orlando Furioso* said of a nobleman, 'Nature made him and then broke the mould', meaning that when he was dead the world would never see his like again.

**Brigade** Like so many *isms*, brigades have changed sides. The British Army has brigades (i.e. a combination of a number of regiments) headed by Brigadiers (originally more correctly Brigadier-Generals, or Brigadiers-General). But the original brigades were bands of brigands (see under TERRORIST) who would have been pursued by a country's regular or official armies. However, after the Spanish Civil War of the 1930s, when there was formed an International Brigade to fight for the republican (i.e. revolutionary) side, the word changed sides again and was taken up by such undefinable LEFTist bodies as the self-styled Red Brigade, generally small groups of persons with fervent ideas and a few bombs, for whose detonation they could CLAIM RESPONSIBILITY by means of anonymous telephone calls. Such 'brigades' cause much consternation and some damage while they exist but like many political student fads usually have a short life.

**Brilliant** See FABULOUS.

**Brit(s)** This now common abbreviation for a Briton or the British is at least as old as the 20th century but has only in recent years (probably since the renewed Irish troubles from the late 1960s) acquired a new pejorative meaning, helped by the way it lends itself to a kind of spitting enunciation. If people have some kind of nationalist axe to grind, dislike Englishmen (at whom it is usually aimed) or just want to be offensive – let them. But in ordinary, neutral use the time and effort saved is hardly worth it. Moreover, those who habitually say 'Brits' are usually quick to complain if someone talks about JAPS or 'nigs' or 'frogs'.

**Broad** American, slightly derogatory, disrespectful or derisive term for a girl, from the German *Braut*=bride. (Some have suggested a corruption of the old English *bawd*, but this is not very convincing, as corruptions usually shorten, not lengthen, words). Like the English word 'tart', a broad is likely to denote a woman of low morals. When Frank Sinatra wanted to record the song *The Road to Mandalay*, Mrs Elsie Bambridge, the copyright-holder and daughter of Rudyard Kipling (who wrote the words), refused to grant him permission unless he, Sinatra, promised to restore the word 'girl' which he had substituted with 'broad'. Americans profess to be confused or amused when they hear Englishmen talk about having holidays 'on the broads' – the colloquial and almost universal abbreviation of the Broadlands, a watery district in East Anglia famous for its scenery, wildlife and sailing.

**Broadsheets** The 'quality' newspapers, as opposed to the smaller-format TABLOIDS.

**Broiling** British cooks have long abandoned the old-fashioned word broiling, meaning to char, or grill with fire – possibly so as to avoid confusion with 'boiling', which means heating in a liquid. Americans, however, have retained both broiling and boiling, using the former where an English person would say 'grilling'. The expression 'It's boiling-hot today' is really a corruption of 'broiling-hot'.

**Brownie** In Britain a brownie can be a popular, small, box-shaped camera introduced by the Kodak Company in the 1930s (now obsolete but remembered fondly). For other meanings, see Colour Supplement.

**Bubbly** Tabloidism for champagne. This is usually either quaffed, downed or knocked back (as newsmen themselves treat their drink?) or, when more genteel drinking is indicated, sipped.

**Budget** Now a commercial euphemism for 'cheap', as in budget fares, budget records, budget shoes, etc. But the word has undergone many changes. When the Chancellor of the Exchequer each year holds up the battered old red briefcase before he reveals his budget, it is the budget we see, for it originally meant a receptacle, from French *bougette*, a little leather bag. Early forms were many and various, and it is sheer chance that we do not now speak of the chancellor's bugget, booget or bogget. Among its older meanings was 'the leathern socket for retaining the butt of a carbine', which in a language as full of double meanings as English soon acquired an obscene one. Henry Purcell towards the end of the 17th century wrote a song beginning:

*As Roger last night to Jenny lay close*
*He pulled out his Budget and gave her a dose.*
*Ye tickling no sooner kind Jenny did find*
*But with laughing she purged both before and behind* . . . etc.

**Bulge**   The sudden increase in the birth-rate which occurred after the return home of servicemen at the end of the Second World War. This figurative bulge worked its way through the education system, making additional demands on schools, universities and jobs. More recent, smaller but no less noticeable bulges have occurred following widespread power-failures (e.g. a calamitous one in New York) which left a bored, television-dependent population with nothing to do except to go to bed.

**Bulldozing**   The original word would strike fear in the hearts of American negro slaves, for it meant a cruel and ferocious flogging. Originally written 'bulldosing', it described 'a dose of the bull-hide whip'. The *Spectator* of 26th April 1879 wrote: 'They (i.e. the negroes) are deprived by terrorism of their votes; (and) are bulldozed, that is, severely flogged, for any exhibition of independence.' (Notice also the early use of TERRORISM.)

**Bumf**   Not 'bumpf' or 'bumph' but, strictly, 'bumf', i.e. an abbreviation of 'bum fodder', the slang term of what is commonly but inaccurately called 'toilet paper'. The usage goes back to the 19th century, and must be classed as a euphemism. Bum-food, incidentally, is not related to bumf, but was the older American term for what is now JUNK food – that is, food fit only for bums, or tramps. Incidentally, all lovers of words should study the exhaustive *bum* section of the OED.

**Buoyant**   In financial jargon, a euphemism for high prices. When commodities are said to be buoyant, things so described are sure to become dear.

**-burger**   Favourite fast-food noun-forming suffix which started with the Hamburger (very remotely based on an item of food once popular in Hamburg, a flattened meat-ball – see also WEENIES) combinable with almost any word suggesting a sliced bread-roll filled with whatever modified the -burger: cheeseburger, sausageburger, chickenburger, etc. (with or without a hyphen) and even, for a slice of bread between two other slices of bread, a burger-burger.

**Burglarise** American for the perfectly adequate and shorter English verb to burgle. I include it here as a cautionary example of an ugly and insidious trend, e.g. hospitalise, concertise, tenderise, etc. It comes naturally to Americans via the German suffix -ieren.

**Business as usual** A slogan which is now part of the language but which is one of the less memorable phrases coined by Winston Churchill. He said it on 9th November 1940, in a speech at the Guildhall, London, after the city had suffered heavy bombing by the Germans: 'The maxim of the British people is "Business as Usual".' Within hours chalked notices bearing these three words began to go up all over bomb-damaged premises, public, business and domestic. See also CALLING CARD for a euphemism of canine 'business'.

**Business girls** What prostitutes euphemistically call themselves. They describe their customers as PUNTERS.

**Bussing** A comparatively recent change in meaning. In the 1960s in America it meant 'taking children from one area to school in another so as to mix those from different racial and social backgrounds', and, more recently, it has come to mean taking passengers in general from one place to another by bus. Previously, and for centuries, it meant 'kissing in a rather lecherous manner'. Robert Herrick explained it perfectly in 1628:

*Kissing and bussing differ both in this,*
*We busse our wantons, but our wives we kisse.*

**-busters** Title cliché suffix, which probably came into wider, non-slang use after the press insisted on calling Rhodesian sanctions-breaking 'sanctions-busting'. Then came various entertainments like *Ghostbusters*, and shops selling cheap goods called themselves 'pricebusters'.

**Butskellism** A combination of the names of the Conservative politician R. A. Butler (1902–1982) and the Labour leader Hugh Gaitskell (1906–1963). The *ism* resulted from the name 'Mr Butskell', coined by a political commentator writing in the *Spectator*, who described this person as 'a composite of the present Chancellor and the previous one ...' meaning that in spite of their being political opponents Butler and Gaitskell advocated much the same policies. Butskellism is a rare quality in British politics, where government and opposition parties all too seldom give each other credit for measures they themselves would encourage/oppose when in government/opposition. See also THATCHERISM.

**Buzz word** A newly fashionable word which is on everybody's lips or at any rate on those whose owners are susceptible to the latest in slang or jargon, who busily buzz it about. The OED defines as a Buzzer 'A private obtruder of tales', quoting from *Hamlet*: 'Her brother wants not buzzers to infect his eare with pestilent speeches ...'. The most common and fastest-spreading buzz words emanate from the COMMUNITY industry, via academic sociological theorists.

**By** The American use of 'by' is slowly creeping into English, e.g. 'dropping by', for a brief and unannounced visit; or 'It's OK by me'. It is a HOBSON-JOBSON formation, from the German *bei*.

**By virtue of** Three words that often replace the short, simple 'because'.

# C

**Cache** French for a hiding-place, and (e.g. a cache of arms) nearly always preferred in media language to one of the many available English words.

**Calling-card** Euphemism for dogs' excrement or 'business'. See WALKIES.

**Camp** Old meaning: a place where people are lodged in tents or other hurriedly-constructed accommodation. Later, when effeminate actors affected a real or feigned homosexual style this became known as 'camping it up'. But the most recent twist in the fortunes of the word comes in descriptions of places in the Lebanon: urban areas of town houses and tower-blocks made from that traditional middle-eastern building-material, reinforced concrete, but showing the depredations of years of internecine Arab fighting. Such places are unaccountably described as 'camps'.

**Can I help you?** Unless said with great solicitousness this common expression no longer represents an offer of help but means 'What the hell do you think you are doing here?'

**Capitalism** Capitalists – from the Latin word for 'head' – were first so named during the time of the French Revolution . . . and later decapitated, many of them. As a political term it did not generally take hold until the middle of the 19th century, and was consolidated as a communist/SOCIALIst term of abuse only after Marx and Engels had had their way with it. The Russians and their FELLOW-TRAVELLERS like to combine and reinforce it with another word of NEGATIVE associations, making 'capitalist-imperialist' (to which can be added a whole menagerie of hyenas, running dogs, etc.). As soon as it became a political vogue word it started to drive out the once fashionable expression of excellence, 'capital!' – which, like 'top hole!' now sounds dated and strange. Capitalism has become less of a dirty word amongst British socialists than it used to be: many Labour politicians are shareholders in commerce and industry and trades unions invest their pensions funds to gain the best returns on their capital or buy works of art for no other reason than to put them in store and watch them increase in value. Thus capitalism is in all but name practised by even the staunchest anti-capitalists. Mrs Margaret Thatcher, as prime minister, vowed to 'make Britain a nation of capitalists' by selling off nationalised industries (some said selling them to the people who already owned them) and to a great extent succeeded, especially as many of the new captalists also became new land-owners when they privatised their former council houses. And in 1986 the Labour leader Neil Kinnock advocated much the same thing in the form of a Labour-sponsored form of share-holding capitalism which he euphemised as 'social ownership'. Over the years the pronunciation of the word has changed: it is now nearly always *cap*'t'list, whereas older people used to say ca*pit*alist, in four syllables and with the stress on the pit – a pronunciation Mr Kinnock would probably have considered (THE) PITS.

**Caring** The vogue-description (usually self-description) of workers of the WELFARE STATE. Often TWINNED in a jingling reduplication with -sharing, perhaps from an advertising-SLOGAN invented for a CHAIN of shops, 'Your Caring Sharing Co-op'.

**Cat** A word with many slang meanings in reference to humans, and some go back to the 18th century and earlier. In its modern sense, it originated in the negro and creole jazz musicians' slang of New Orleans of the early 20th century. Cats may be hep, hip or cool and have many other attributes considered praiseworthy in the ALTERNATIVE society.

**Centre** Modern euphemism for a shop. Toy shops have become Toy Centres, sweet shops Sweet Centres, travel agents (and railway booking offices) Travel Centres – and even the old British Employment Exchange is now a Job Centre. But at the same time it has become common for makers of sound-reproducing equipment to describe their products as Music Centres, e.g. when it contains a radio as well as one or more ways of playing/recording, such as cassette tape, disc and/or compact-disc – a kind of modern RADIOGRAM. In addition, some schools and other educational or recreational institutions describe premises where musical activities are carried on as their Music Centre. But the

**Chain store** is not a 'Chain Centre', or a place where chains are sold, but the American name for a HIGH STREET shop with many branches – the very opposite of a CORNER SHOP.

**Chair** No longer does this denote an inanimate object with four legs and a seat. It is the new word, untainted by sexism, for a CHAIRMAN. Before the Age of the GLC (deceased) and its lunatic concern with trivia, people happily addressed a chairman, a Mr

Chairman or even a Madam Chairman, without danger of gender-confusion. Then for a time, before things started to get frantic in the (largely GLC-generated) discrimination industry, Chairperson was considered acceptable – though not Chairwoman, because of its uncomfortable closeness to 'charwoman'. Now 'chair' is the normal term, usually among speakers and writers who are full of AWARENESS and/or CONSCIOUSNESS. Not even when one of them said, during the course of a heated debate, 'The chair hasn't got a leg to stand on' did they see any absurdity; and they think nothing of addressing a woman as 'Madam Chair'. Papers like the *Guardian, New Society,* and the *New Statesman* appear to have written these walking, talking bits of furniture into their house rules. And certain men who have every right to describe themselves as chairmen will demonstrate sisterly solidarity by nonsensically saying 'I'm the chair of the board of governors' (not yet, note well, 'governesses').

**Chairman**   A substitute for the ancient office of mayor (in some cities lord mayor) which was introduced during the late 1970s and early 80s by certain LOONY left local authorities, e.g. Liverpool, on the model of the now discredited Chairman Mao of communist China – and retained even after China began to turn CAPITALIST. This abolition could be dismissed as a harmless, unimportant and temporary aberration, a mere hiatus in the history of towns and cities that dates back to the middle ages, were it not often combined with the mindless destruction of ancient silver, ceremonial coaches, and regalia. When the Liverpool lord mayoralty was briefly restored in 1987 it was found that many of the mayoral appurtenances had disappeared. The coach was in a museum and its horses had been sent to the knacker's yard.

**(The) challenge**   See BECAUSE IT IS THERE.

**Character**   From a Greek and Latin word meaning an engraving-tool. Later the sense was transferred to mean the letter, or character, it was used to engrave; and later still, after printing was invented, a character became a piece of printing-type. The figurative and transferred meanings soon proliferated, but anyone now asked to define the meaning of the word would probably think of either a person's qualities ('of good character') or of a character, defined as 'An odd or eccentric person' as early as 1773. In addition to such characters there are chaps (a vulgar abbreviation of the ancient chapman) and fellows. *Punch* was at one period fond of calling people parties ('Collapse of stout party'); and the most up-to-date informal name for a man is guy. A guy was, from 1840, 'a person of grotesque appearance, especially with reference to dress'; but later, towards the end of the century, the word became a standard Americanism for any man. Many stories, narratives and jokes start with the preamble, 'There was this guy . . .'. English policemen tend to speak of persons as elements and doctors and lawyers as cases.

**(The) charts** These play an important role in the life of the modern young, who are kept informed about the JUNK music they are supposed to buy – by an industry run by cynics with the help of a covert PAYOLA system. Even the Beatles achieved their first breakthrough by means of fiddled charts, when their manager, Brian Epstein, bought huge quantities of their first record, thereby putting them into the charts, after which he had no difficulty in selling the stockpiles in his record shops. Thus are the young BRAINWASHED.

**Check** American for what most English people still call a bill, e.g. in a restaurant. Thus Englishmen might pay their bill with a note (long may they continue to do so) while Americans pay their check with a bill (e.g. a dollar bill). A cheque was originally the counterfoil of an exchequer, or bank draft. To ask an American waiter for a bill might lead him to suppose you wanted a tip (i.e. a bank-note) from him. The American word comes from the German *Zeche*, meaning consumption. See also FLEXIBLE FRIEND and PLASTIC.

**Chemistry** The art or practice of the chemist; who, in modern usage, might be either a person who sells medicines in his CORNER SHOP or works in a laboratory. Hence it has become customary to use a qualifying prefix e.g. dispensing chemist, research chemist, etc. (HIGH STREET chemists slightly confuse the terminology, as they are really CHAIN STORES that happen to have a department that dispenses medicines). The OED suggests that chemistry was at first probably a contemptuous term, like casuistry, sophistry and palmistry. A new kind of chemistry is the now modish cliché description of – usually unsuccessful – INTER-personal relationships, e.g. the excuse for a quarrel, 'Our chemistry wasn't right'. The entrepreneur-entertainer David Frost in a much-quoted statement in the mid-1980s promised good 'sexual chemistry' between presenters when he helped to found a new television company. But before many weeks had passed the presenters' chemical reaction to each other had formed an explosive mixture, and the company itself nearly went bankrupt.

**Chinaman**  Old word for a Chinese man or Chinese person, now considered slightly derogatory – although Chinese people, who are not at all touchy about what others call them, don't seem to care either way. See below, and also CRISPY and JAP.

**Chinee**  Facetious, bogus-singular back-formation from 'Chinese', which is, from its sound, for this purpose taken to be a plural. Hence used as a facetious word for a Chinese person. 'Chinee'-based silly jokes include the numerous and once popular 'Confucius he say' anecdotes (e.g. 'Confucius he say rape impossible because woman with skirts up run faster than man with trousers down'). See also CRISPY and SOFTLY SOFTLY.

**Chinless wonder**  Working-class term of abuse aimed at educated persons of the YUPPIE or even HOORAY HENRY type, based on the false assumption that the size or strength of a person's chin is an indication of his or her character and determination. It is true that weak people are generally *caricatured* as chinless (and wearing spectacles) but reality does not bear out these cliché generalisations. In 1986, when the Labour Party had gained a reputation for coming second or third in elections, a 'strong' Labour candidate won a parliamentary election without the benefit of any chin whatsoever. One can only hope that he will reach high office, and see what the cartoonists make of his chinlessness. I suspect there is a confusion between a metaphorical spinelessness or even bonelessness, traditional descriptions for those alleged to lack courage, character or resolve. In 1931 Winston Churchill, during a debate in the House of Commons, said of James Ramsay MacDonald, 'I remember when I was a child being taken to the celebrated Barnum Circus. The exhibit which I most desired to see was the one described as ''The

Boneless Wonder''. My parents judged that the spectacle would
be too revolting for my youthful eyes, and I have waited fifty
years to see the Boneless Wonder sitting on the Treasury Bench.'

**(A) Chip on the shoulder**   A display of defiance and over-
sensitivity, or quickness to take offence, caused perhaps but not
excused by the condition known pseudo-scientifically as an
'inferiority complex'. The OED cites a remarkably implausible-
sounding explanation of 1830 taken from the *Long Island
Telegraph*, 'When two churlish boys were determined to fight,
a chip would be placed on the shoulder of one, and the other
[was] demanded to knock it off at his peril'. The expression is
claimed to be American but now survives chiefly in British-English
slang.

**Chop suey**   See SPAGHETTI.

**Christian name**   See FORENAME.

**(The) City**   Apart from the ordinary meanings, a shorthand way
of referring to British financial institutions, originally those in the
immediate neighbourhood of the Bank of England and the Stock
Exchange, situated in the ancient heart of London, i.e. the true
INNER CITY.

**Claimants**   Euphemism for the unemployed, i.e. those claiming
unemployment benefit. See also UNWAGED, REDUNDANT and their
various cross-references.

**Claiming responsibility**   One of the curiosities of speech in
today's violent world. The perpetrators of outrages, such as the
murder of innocent people by bombing or gunfire, later
telephone a newspaper, radio station or the police and, as the
news jargon always puts it, *claim* responsibility, as though it were
something to claim credit for. Many people feel that *admit* would
be more appropriate. On the other hand, if a DEMO or other protest
gets out of hand and turns into a riot or results in the looting of
homes and shops, or even death or injury, the organisers always
*dis*claim responsibility, invariably putting the blame on unnamed
'outsiders'. This was always so during the miners' and
newspapermen's riots during the mid-1980s.

**Class** This apparently unequivocal word has changed its meaning and become a politicised tool of the class war, even its pronunciation turned into a weapon ranging from the elongated, drawling, upper-class 'cl-a-ss' to the clipped, working-class 'cluss' (where it is usually combined with words such as 'struggle', 'distinction' or 'war'). But its sense has been blunted. As I hurry for a second-class seat on the INTER-City express I often pass one of our Merseyside MPs of the LOONY LEFT, already comfortably seated with his lady-wife and, fighting the class war on my behalf from a first-class compartment. And the sometime LOONY Deputy Leader of Liverpool City Council during his brief but disastrous incumbence became famous for his guttural 'cluss' utterances, rallying the flat-capped 'wairkers' while sharply attired in what used to be described as a 'hundred guinea suit' but is now considerably more expensive.

**Clawback** The state gives and the state takes away; and clawback is overdramatised JOURNO slang for what it takes back again, e.g. by taxing family-allowances.

**Cleansing operative** Municipalese GENTEELISM for a road-sweeper, though in some LOONY local authorities this is the preferred appellation for a dustman. The honourable calling of Cleansing Operatives, alias road-sweepers and dustmen, has at last been dignified by the formation of a Livery Company in the City of London, and received its Letters Patent from the Lord Mayor in January 1987. The new body is called The Worshipful Company of Environmental Cleaners. So far there has been no noticeable difference on the streets and pavements of London, which are as dirty, litter-strewn and infested as ever with mountains of overflowing plastic refuse bags. See also ENVIRONMENTAL CLEANER.

**Clever, these Chinese/Japs!** A catch-phrase once commonly heard in Britain, said sardonically of any small, probably mechanical and perhaps ingenious but home-made, contrivance. It arose from the once notorious capacity shown by Far Eastern engineers for copying Western inventions. But now, at any rate as far as the JAPS are concerned and certainly in the field of consumer electronics and optics (not to mention sheer industriousness), it is often the Far East which leads and the West that follows. After all, the word TYCOON was given to us by the East.

**Climate of opinion**  The popular GROUNDSWELL among the GRASS ROOTS, usually discernible only to politicians and political commentators.

**Clitch**  Facetious pronunciation of 'cliché', derived from a famous statement by Ernest Bevin (1881–1951) who in the house of Commons described the speech of an opponent as 'clitch after clitch after clitch'. Bevin was a politician not noted for his intelligence, and this kind of mispronunciation is always a sure sign of someone (e.g. a journalist or politician) who reads about matters he has never heard discussed. The resulting mispronunciations are now common among radio journalists after CRASH research in the reference-books.

**Closet**  Adjectival noun denoting secret beliefs or practices, like closet communist, closet homosexual, etc. Originally invented in America, where a closet is a cupboard, not (as in Britain) a euphemism for a LAVATORY or TOILET (which are, of course, themselves euphemisms). See COMING OUT.

**Cloud cuckoo land**  A fanciful place which exists only in the imagination; or, a place where, in the opinion of the less gullible, someone believes there obtain ideal social or political conditions. From a story in Aristophanes's comedy, *The Birds*. It appears also to be inhabited by many radio and television interviewees – at least according to their interlocutors, who often ask, 'But aren't you living in cloud cuckoo land?'

**Cloud nine**  A place of extreme happiness, situated perhaps OVER THE MOON. Americans, however, say they are 'on cloud seven', epecially when in a narcotic trance or 'on a high'. Meteorologists explain the expression with the information that the highest clouds are about eight miles high; therefore 'cloud nine' is even higher. See also SICK AS A PARROT.

**Cold war**  Hostilities between nations, usually the Soviet Union and the West, that stop short of actual fighting (which, by extension, is known as a 'hot war'). According to William Safire, the term was 'minted by Herbert Bayard Swope, publicist, three-time winner of the Pulitzer Prize, and occasional speechwriter for elder statesman Barnard Baruch ...' who used it in a speech in 1947.

**(The) .... collection**  A commercial jargon description of goods which is intended to make these sound more attractive, desirable and saleable; perhaps related to the pretentious name GALLERY for a shop – thereby giving the impression that buyers are being offered works of art.

**Collective**  Nineteenth-century SOCIALISTS courageously advocated 'collectivism' (an early *ism*, incidentally). The Soviet collective farms boosted the use of the word, although British farmers who adopted some of these ideas preferred to call the practice 'co-operative farming'. Now, however, 'collective' is used far more widely as a noun than an adjective; and anything described as 'a collective' is sure to be some sort of manifestation of trendy subculture, e.g. militant feminism. When a group of prostitutes banded together to fight for their rights, the result was – inevitably – the London Collective of Prostitutes.

**Colonels**  When foreign military men seize power by organising a revolt they curiously seem to have or adopt (and retain) the rank of colonel. So it was in Greece 'under the colonels' and elsewhere before and since. This is strange, as they wield absolute power and could just as easily make themselves generals or field marshals. Indeed an African cannibal ruler called Bokassa ordered a crown and a golden throne from Europe and, as there was no-one of higher rank than himself, and in imitation of Napoleon Bonaparte, crowned *himself* Emperor and declared his BANANA republic 'The Central African Empire'.

**Coming out**  Few expressions better illustrate recent changes in English social conditions and attitudes. Less than a generation or so ago, the marriageable daughters of rich and/or noble families would be Presented at Court, i.e. shown off to the Queen or other members of the royal family at special parties given for that sole purpose by the court. Young women so presented thus made their social debut and were known as debutantes (or more often, colloquially, 'debs'). The practice differed only in detail from the cattle fair, and rigorous checks were made by the matrons-in-charge as to the financial suitability of possible male partners (see FU). However, the word 'deb' is now seldom heard, and 'coming out' has moved from being Queen's English to 'queens' English', i.e. homosexual slang. Coming out now means out of the CLOSET, i.e. a frank declaration of homosexuality on the part of the person emerging into the open. The appropriate slogan is Proud to be Gay. But as I write this, and the MEDIA are full of the perils of AIDS, many 'gays' are rapidly returning to their closets.

**Commercial television** Surely this is the correct name for what the commercial television and radio companies like to euphemise as 'independent' television and radio, since they are totally dependent on their advertisers and seldom risk offending them for fear of losing their custom and revenue. Although the independence and impartiality of the BBC is constantly, and healthily, questioned by political parties (which employ researchers with stop-watches to check relative exposure, alleged bias, etc.), the corporation is far more independent of outside commercial or political pressures than any other radio or television organisation in the world. See also SOAPS.

**Commfu** See SNAFU.

**Commissar** The Russian equivalent – in a very loose sense – of the Nazi *Gauleiter*. The word came into being during the Russian revolution of 1917 (at first anglicised in the English press as 'commissary') and although taken from the German *Kommissär* it predates Nazism by about 15 years. Whereas a *Gauleiter* was in effect the *Leiter* (director) of a *Gau* (district), Soviet commissars, also People's Commissars, could be created almost at the drop of an official's cap. They were responsible for keeping the populace in order and indoctrinated with the appropriate PROPAGANDA. However, the Soviets in 1946 decided to rename commissars 'ministers', but whatever new and euphemistic titles you give to bogeymen they still remain bogeymen. In facetious English usage *Gauleiter* and commissar are descriptions derisively applied to persons alleged to be officious and self-important (usually by those too young to know what the real culprits could be like). See also DISINFORMATION, PEOPLE'S, PROLETARIANS.

**Commitment** See MOTIVATION.

**Common law wife** No statute exists under English common law that can make a mistress or live-in girl-friend into a wife. One might equally well call a nut-cutlet a common-law steak. This ludicrous euphemism is indeed common but is certainly not lawful – a media invention pure and simple. Curiously enough it is less often applied to men: common-law husbands are rare. Nor has anyone ever suggested a qualifying time-scale. How long does a girl-friend have to be in residence in order to be accorded this bogus title? A year, a week or a night? More curiously still, the term is now used even by judges, barristers and solicitors during court proceedings. In Scotland, however, mistresses may obtain some form of legal recognition as 'partners of habit and repute'. See also SINGLE PARENT FAMILY.

**Communications corps** Some years ago a trade organisation of English newsagents decided grandly to rename their delivery boys and girls 'Members of the Communications Corps', at the same time instituting one of the OF THE YEAR awards for them. This made everyone feel better – except the newspaper delivery boys and girls, who have to get up just as early and remain as underpaid and overworked as before. See also DELIVERY OFFICER.

**Community** The great buzz-word of idealist-SOCIALIST thinking of the mid-20th century (indeed of all fashionable *ism* supporters now active) and one of the key prefix-words of the WELFARE STATE. Put it in front of almost any other word (Community Action, Community Politics, Community Policing, Community Health, Community Relations, Community Schools, etc., etc., *ad infinitum et nauseam*) and you will suggest a wonderful unity of purpose and communal civic spirit – a suggestion which a glance at the places where the term is most used will prove to be false. The pages of the *Guardian, New Society,* the *New Statesman* and similar publications are full of advertisements offering positions with 'community' titles. The word is, however, by no means confined to the LEFTist vocabulary: in the late 1980s, as the abolition of the domestic rate on householders is being prepared, the

THATCHERITE government, too, is proposing to call its replacement a 'Community Tax'. See also NEIGHBOURHOOD, and below.

**Community leader**  In Britain it is customary for leaders to be elected. The exception seems to be the nebulous post of 'community leader', now almost invariably a spokesman for non-white people. British Jews, who have lived in this country peacefully for centuries as a religious, cultural and ETHNIC minority (though not without suffering discrimination at times), have had spokesmen but can manage without community leaders.

**Commuter**  A useful import from the USA which during the last 25 years or so has been happily adopted into British English. H. L. Mencken in *The American Language* (Knopf, 1979), defines it as 'a season-ticket-holder' – presumably therefore one who travels by public transport. Now, however, a commuter is taken to be any regular, daily traveller who goes to and from work by any form of transport he chooses.

**Competitive**  Commercial, MARKETING and advertising jargon meaning cheap (a word which perhaps has acquired too many other connotations, e.g. 'cheap and nasty'). Competitive prices are, of course, a good thing for CONSUMERISM, but when the goods themselves are described as competitive, usage has got out of hand.

**Concern** A vogue-suffix of the WELFARE STATE and its ancillary or complementary organisations and pressure-groups, many of them voluntary and most of them laudable, e.g. Age Concern, Education Concern, Health Concern, etc.

**Condom** From the middle of 1986, as AIDS began to reach epidemic proportions among certain groups and began to threaten the population at large, the condom was suddenly on everyone's lips. It is word of doubtful origin, meaning the rubber contraceptive sheath, colloquially a French letter and commercially a Durex. It has been claimed that the article was named after its alleged inventor, a Doctor Condom, Condum or Cundum who in the 18th century devised one from animal membranes (e.g. fish-skin). The purpose was then to protect the man from venereal disease, not the woman from unwanted pregnancy. But no such doctor has been found in the medical records (such as were kept). There is, however, a town called Condom in France (you can't miss it – south-east of Bordeaux and a few miles from a place called Sore) and if a connection were established it would make the French letter really French, just as the bayonet comes from Bayonne. However, a recent article in *History Today* revealed that in the eighteenth century hundreds of condoms or French letters were exported from England to France for the use of Louis XV. So perhaps the French name *capote anglais* is more seminal than counter-abusive.

**Conference** See SEMINAR.

**(The) .... Connection** Media and advertising cliché, originating from a film called *The French Connection*.

**Consciousness** An important quality allegedly necessary to be possessed by members of minority groups – even more important than the equally nebulous AWARENESS – gay consciousness, black consciousness, Irish consciousness, etc. So widespread is the quest for consciousness now that the political prisoners adopted by Amnesty International and named

'Prisoners of Conscience' are quite unselfconsciously referred to by some as 'Prisoners of Consciousness'.

**Consensus** Almost always a pretentious word for 'agreement'.

**Consultancy** 'I've set up a consultancy' is often a euphemism of the recently unemployed, their way of saying they are BETWEEN JOBS or REDUNDANT. However, the title consultant surgeon or physician denotes a certain rank in the medical profession, and consultant engineers*, architects, etc. are also long-established legitimate users of the consultancy title. But there is no doubt that some consultancies work on the principle that it is often easier to advise others on how to do their work than to do it oneself. For example, a group of tomcats would often meet on the rooftops at night, pursuing females and generally getting into mischief, when they noticed that one of their number had been absent for several days. After a while he returned to the group, heavily bandaged in his hindquarters. He said, 'I'm afraid I won't be coming out with you any more, lads. I've set up a consultancy.' See also PREUSED.

**Consumer** Euphemism for the customer.

**Contemporary** In art, decorative design, architecture, music, etc., this means present-day, or modern. It is always worth asking, 'Contemporary with what or whom?'

**Contender** Boxers' euphemism for one of their number, an expression they copy from commentators' jargon (see STOP). It is also one of the rare 'intellectual' words regularly used by sportsmen not otherwise noted for their wide vocabulary, and punch-drunk 'fighters' with hardly a couple of brain-cells left to rub together may often be heard talking about 'encountering a world-class contender'.

**Controlled landfill** Municipal euphemism for the official dumping of rubble and refuse. The resulting tip is often euphemised as a 'Household Waste Amenity Point', where the dustmen, or 'Sanitary Wardens', tip the domestic rubbish.

---

*Some call themselves 'consulting' engineers. Whom do they consult?

**Conversazione**  See CONFERENCE.

**Corner shop**  The standard neologism for a small, privately-owned shop. It is thus described even if it is in the middle of a row of other shops on the HIGH STREET. Conversely, big shops, even if situated on corner sites of side-streets, are always called High Street shops. Banks and building societies are also given the almost invariable High Street prefix. This is standard journalistic practice, though ordinary people have not yet taken to it. But they will, in time.

**Corporate advertising**  The advertising, usually on television or by means of expensive full-page announcements in the BROADSHEETS, of entire industries instead of, as is more usual, individual firms. The advertisements are often issued by state monopolies, like British Rail(ways) or the electricity boards, which makes such a practice even more pointless. The consumer not only does not have the choice of travelling by a different railway system or using private electricity but in addition has no say in the costs of the advertising – for which he ultimately pays.

**Country fresh**  One of the food-manufacturers' hyperboles, the examples too many and too familiar to be worth including here. Also FARM FRESH.

**Coup**  See PUTSCH.

**Crash**  Adjectival noun to denote haste, usually in response to pressure. The OED Supplement defines it as something 'undertaken with rapidity or intensive effort'. Newspapers have seriously reported things like 'a crash programme for training commercial pilots'.

**Cred**  Short for 'credibility', as in 'street cred'. This is something every trendy young person thinks he needs – even those who do not know what the word means and have been educationally so neglected that they have no credo of any sort. Cred ranks with all the other post-GLC qualities demanded in social services advertisements, like MOTIVATION and its unlovely, objectless mates, though it arrived in the vocabulary later.

**Crescendo** The cliché expression 'reaching a crescendo' serves as an AWFUL warning to anyone who lightly appropriates professionals' shop-talk he does not understand. When used by journalists and others it is intended to suggest a great climax, a FORTE, whereas, as every musician knows, the point in the ORCHESTRATION where music *reaches* a *crescendo* is usually marked *piano* or *pianissimo* (i.e. soft), so as to give the impending *crescendo* a starting-point and the player the opportunity of making the music louder by degrees. As every composer knows, there is little point in asking players who are already playing *fortissimo* to make a *crescendo*. See also LOW KEY.

**Crispy** A nonce-word much used by the food industry and introduced either by Chinese restaurant keepers who thought there was such a word, or, facetiously, by those who think that words sound more CHINEE if they have an -ee (or -y) ending; as in 'Softly, softly catchee monkey'.

**Culling** Widely thought to be a euphemism for killing, because of the annual harrowing press coverage of the 'seal-cull'. Seals eat fish, and fishermen try to reduce the seal-population; and they do it in a way that is bloody and apparently ceremonial, with the entire population of some islands taking part. But 'culling' really means 'choosing': in truth, fishermen tend to 'choose' the small, defenceless baby-seals. Shakespeare and other poets sang of 'a nosegay of culled flowers'; and in an earlier meaning, 'to cull' was also used in the sense of 'to hug'. A real Judas word, therefore, turning round from hugging to killing.

**Culture shock** An alleged difficulty or inability to get used to different surroundings – nearly always used facetiously and having little or no connection with culture.

**(Like the) curate's egg** A common catch-phrase with the usually unspoken qualification, 'good in parts'. It comes from a famous *Punch* cartoon by George du Maurier of 9th November 1895 (see opposite).

**Curry** (Prefix) see SPAGHETTI.

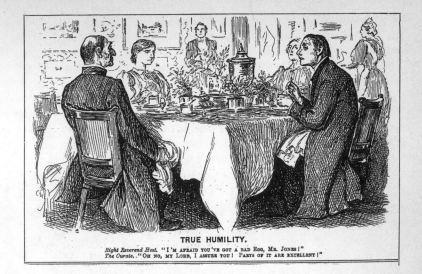

**TRUE HUMILITY.**

*Right Reverend Host.* "I 'M AFRAID YOU 'VE GOT A BAD EGG, MR. JONES!"
*The Curate.* "OH NO, MY LORD, I ASSURE YOU! PARTS OF IT ARE EXCELLENT!"

# D

**Dedication** In the repetitive jargon of radio disc jockeys this means a gramophone record (or an ALBUM track) requested by a listener together with a birthday, anniversary, etc. message to a friend or relation to be read out by the disc-jockey. But on COMMERCIAL radio or television such a message must not be confused with a MESSAGE, which please see.

**Delhi belly** See AZTEC TWO-STEP.

**Delivery officer** In 1987 the Post Office decided to confer on the friendly old British postman this grand euphemistic title, thereby putting him on a level with the members of the COMMUNICATIONS CORPS.

**Demo(nstration)** The older meaning of this Latin-based word for the action of making something evident by proof, or showing how it is done, might be better expressed with the full word, 'demonstration', and left to the kind of 'demonstrators' who show how wonderfully effective some new product is. The abbreviation 'demo' could then be kept for political or pseudo-political people who feel they have a grievance and wish to demonstrate it noisily. One would then be less likely to get the wrong impression, e.g. when reading in the newspapers that 'There have been demonstrations by active homosexuals in St Peter's, Rome'. See also RENTA-.

**Democratic** From the Greek words for 'rule by the people' but much debased and made either meaningless or twisted to mean the very opposite. Countries which proclaim themselves 'people's democracies' are without exception places where the people have little democratic say in their destiny, though a great deal of time is spent on democratic charades, e.g. 'PEOPLE'S courts' or universal franchise – at single-candidate elections.

**Deprived** Welfare state euphemism for poor. Also DISADVANTAGED and UNDERPRIVILEGED, not to mention the UNWAGED, who alas are always with us.

**Designer** An adjectival noun denoting alleged desirability, and a word whose over-use is becoming as obtrusive as that of EXECUTIVE and the (ONGOING) SITUATION did during the 1970s and 80s. The craze began when dress-designers (at first mostly French) discovered that they could increase their profits if they diversified by selling scents and perfumes under their names. Thus were invented 'designer perfumes'. Almost anything can now be sold with the 'designer' prefix, but things soon came full-circle back to the clothes-designers, with designer jeans and designer handbags. In spite of this cachet, products sold with the 'designer' description are usually mass-produced in factories. The big stores also follow the practice but call it more honestly 'own-brand' selling.

**Designer stubble** This was made fashionable in 1986 by pop-music entertainers, who turned their aversion to shaving (and doubtless to soap-and-water generally) into their particular 'thing', always appearing in public with two or three days' stubble on their faces. Nothing spreads as fast as a fad introduced by a pop entertainer, and makers of electric razors soon took advantage of it by making and selling Designer Stubble Razors. These (negating all previous claims of efficiency) keep the facial hair at a certain desirable length of controlled scruffiness, thus

avoiding the tiresome need for being clean-shaven once or twice
a week.

**Destabilisation**   A COLD WAR euphemism, being a way of
describing United States interference (usually organised by the
Central Intelligence Agency) in the internal affairs of a state whose
regime is disapproved of by the American government. The idea
was, however, not invented by the Americans, only the
euphemism. The Soviet Union, for example, had been
clandestinely interfering in other countries' affairs for many years
previously but, being dictatorships controlling information, they
have never had a word for it because they do not recognise its
existence. However, it should be said that many countries' affairs
are well worth destabilising.

**Détente**   An improvement in relations between countries, or a
thaw in the chilly relations between nations known as the COLD
WAR. The opposite of détente is escalation, which confusingly may
(in extreme cases) turn the temperature simile upside-down, by
reversing the 'thaw' – not into something cooler but a 'hot war'.
There should, strictly, be an acute accent on the first é, but our
journalists and their typesetters seldom bother about such
niceties.

**Deviant**   Usually an abbreviation of 'sexual deviant', generally
but not necessarily homosexual. It is a NEGATIVE word, and not
one favoured by deviants themselves, who are constantly
searching for new euphemisms, such as the sadly abused 'gay',
or sinister ones like PAEDOPHILE.

**Dialling**   This word for the action of selecting a telephone number
when making a call is said by some to be an archaism, as modern
telephones have a key-pad instead of a dial, and the keys are
pressed, not chosen by revolving the telephone dial. The
Americans, who have had key-pads longer than the British, use
the ugly expression 'punching a number', but there is no need
for such a change: the word dial does not mean 'round like a
clock' but comes from the Latin *dies*, a day, and was therefore
an inaccuracy to begin with. There is no harm in continuing to
dial our friends. After all, we would not wish to punch, or even

press, them. And we still 'pull the chain' on the TOILET long after
the disappearance of the overhead flushing cistern.

**Differential** The time-honoured belief of the British worker,
however SOCIALIST his leanings, beliefs and opinions, and however
much he condemns ELITISM in others, that his job deserves a higher
wage than his colleagues'. This is soundly-based in the ancient
and respectable guilds and craftsmen's unions, but after the
industrial prosperity following the Second World War the fight
for differentials turned into a spate of countless who-does-what
strikes from which neither the trades union movement nor the
country has yet recovered – though the realities of unemployment
in THATCHERITE Britain are bringing many to their senses.

**Dinkies** One of the YUPPIE group of words, an approximate
acronym for a class of newly prosperous, 'upwardly mobile'
persons. Yummies are Young Upwardly Mobile Marxists, and
Dinkies childless husband-and-wife (or live-together) couples
who are both earning salaries, i.e. 'Double Income – No Kids'.

**Diplomat** A two-faced double-dealer, usually a politician or civil
servant who during the course of his work is obliged to be nice
to nasty people, shake hands with blood-sodden dictators and
generally avoid telling the truth in the interest of international
understanding. In other words, he is 'sent to lie abroad for his
country', as Sir Thomas Wotton wrote in a friend's autograph
album in 1604 (when 'to lie' was still a common euphemism for
sleeping or residing and offered a useful double meaning). The
word very appropriately comes from the Greek *diplos*, double.
Wotton was defining an ambassador – who, however, does much
the same thing; and that word comes from the Latin *ambo*, also
meaning double (e.g. one who makes ambivalent, ambiguous
statements, though other explanations are possible); so they are
by the very nature of their appointment professional liars. In
English news usage the diplomat often gets the double description
of 'career diplomat' (though never 'career ambassador'). This is
usually quite unnecessary, except in rare cases, as when a British
prime minister appointed his son-in-law to the post of British
ambassador to the United States. He was certainly not a *career*
diplomat (and, some said, no diplomat) but a career journalist.
Perhaps his father-in-law had read *The Devil's Dictionary* by

Ambrose Bierce (1842–?1914), which defines 'diplomat' as: '(A person) who, having failed to secure an office from the people, is given one by the administration, on condition that he leave the country'. Foreign diplomats to Great Britain traditionally present their credentials at the Court of St James's, and for this they wear morning-dress and may be accorded the courtesy of a ceremonial horse-drawn coach. And some of them present a very incongruous picture indeed.

**Direct mail** Advertisers' jargon-euphemism for what the rest of us know as JUNK Mail. They and the Post Office love it, but many householders are daily bombarded with masses of unsolicited circulars, leaflets, FREE-SHEETS and other exhortations to join this or buy that. The addresses of unfortunate recipients are gleaned from electoral and shareholders' registers and other firms' mailing-lists and customer-registers, which are bought and sold by and to junk-mail practitioners. The resulting MAIL SHOTS are often accompanied by tempting but near-fraudulent offers of 'prizes' and 'free' gifts for those who merely reply (and thus confirm their existence only to find themselves included on yet another list) and who, thanks to computers, are personally addressed in a way that suggests the sender really cares for their wellbeing, comfort and prosperity. Another form of junk advertising is loose advertising leaflets that fall out of magazines. The floors of news-agents' shops are littered with them.

**Dirty mac brigade** This expression now describes sexual perverts, exhibitionists or visitors to sex shows or PORNOGRAPHIC film shows. But a generation or two ago almost all British urban businessmen belonged to the dirty mac fraternity. Indeed, an entire thesis could be written on the BRIT's raincoat. Until the advent of washable fabrics (and the Clean Air Act, which also abolished the famous British 'peasouper' fog), a grimy, greasy, malodorous macintosh was almost the badge of office of the British businessman or civil servant. The fabric used was invariably subfusc, seldom lighter than a dark beige – 'so it won't show the dirt'. You could always immediately identify an American, German, Swiss or Scandinavian tourist by his clean, pale raincoat. But the British dirt did, of course, show; for dry-cleaning was expensive, involved a renewal of the waterproofing impregnation, and was rarely indulged in. It was also before the introduction (and adoption by men) of the under-arm deodorant; so crowded rush-hour steam-trains could be pretty noisome. Another feature of the British mac used to be (on some perhaps still is) the way the side pockets were contrived so that they communicated through a split in the lining with the wearer's other garments beneath it. Through this he could gain access to, say, his trouser-pockets, to find loose change or a handkerchief. Ingenious DEVIANTS like 'flashers' soon realised the possibilities this arrangement offered for their own, private amusements.

**Disabled**  Everything should be done to help persons afflicted with crippling conditions or chronic illnesses, but euphemisms unfortunately do not make them feel any better, and the description 'visually acutely handicapped' does nothing to better the lot of the blind. But now even 'disabled' has proved too strong for some members of Equity, the actors' union, who have passed resolutions about favouring some of their 'differently-abled' members.

**Disadvantaged**  Especially with a qualifying word, e.g. socially disadvantaged, educationally disadvantaged, etc., this is only another word for poor or UNDERPRIVILEGED. In some circles it is not only acceptable but actually fashionable to bandy about the bogus transitive word 'to disadvantage', i.e. actively and consciously to saddle someone with disadvantages.

**Disciplinary tribunal**  A body elected and convened by members of a profession, e.g. doctors, lawyers or architects, to sit in judgment over those considered to have transgressed in some way against their professional or ethical code. See also KANGAROO COURT, SHOW TRIAL.

**Disinformation**  Official (i.e. government-inspired) lies and half-truths issued as statements to the press for further dissemination: in fact, disguised propaganda. The word was first heard in its Russian form, coined, like so many official Soviet words, from German dialectical jargon. COMMISSARS devoted much time and care to the spread of disinformation, but all governments engage in such falsehoods at one time or another. See also PSYCHOLOGICAL WARFARE.

**Dissident** (noun) A newer, more fashionable alternative to the perfectly good old word 'dissenter'. See also BRAINWASHING, GULAG, PSYCHIATRIC HOSPITAL,. REFUSENIK (under -NIK) – but now, in hopes, also GLASNOST.

**Dogs of war** From Shakespeare's famous line in *Julius Caesar*, 'Cry "Havoc" and let slip the dogs of war'. Now a journalistic cliché exclusively reserved for mercenary soldiers, after the title of a book by Frederick Forsyth.

**Domiciliary vist** Euphemism of the WELFARE STATE for what doctors, nurses and their patients always used to be happy to call 'home visits'.

**Do one's own thing** This is defined in the *Longman Dictionary of Contemporary English* (1978 edition) without further explanation as LETTING IT ALL HANG OUT.

**Downtime** A new word taken from – or at any rate spread by – computer jargon, meaning the time a machine is out of action, either because of a malfunction or because there is no work for it.

**Dream ticket** A supposedly unbeatable combination of two political candidates standing (or, in America, running) for office together – the appeal of one – perhaps right-wing – balancing the other, who might be more to the left. Like many such coinages, it is of American origin and (says William Safire in *The New Language of Politics*) was first used in 1967 ('the Reagan and Brooke dream ticket'). The latest alleged dream ticket in British politics was the Kinnock/Hattersley combination, variously described in the press as 'The Welsh Windbag v. the Yorkshire Nosebag' (because of the latter's reputation as an alleged working-class gourmand). It should be explained that in British politics such a 'ticket' is at first adversarial, in that Kinnock and Hattersley both stood *against* each other for election to the leadership of their party, with the winner becoming Leader of the Opposition (i.e. Prime Minister when the party is in power) and the runner-up Deputy Leader (or, almost automatically, Foreign Secretary when in power). In American presidential elections the two legs of a dream ticket are 'running-mates' from

the start, and the secondary participant in the 'dream' is selected
by the presidential candidate and knows his place before he
starts. And again, in Britain, the alleged dream is supposed to be
that of the electorate, who are promised a spectral range of
political opinion and expertise they had never dreamed of. But
many a dream ticket has turned into a nightmare.

**Drive-in** An American concept, now outdated, of customer-
convenience geared to the motor-car, and an extension of the
formerly popular American drive-in cinema. According to many
predictions by architects, planners and sociologists, the BRAVE
NEW WORLD was going to be full of such facilities. A drive-in bank
near where I write this has been driven into – accidentally – by
a lorry; and has also proved a boon to motorised bank robbers,
who can drive in, point their guns at the cashier through the
window, grab the cash, and drive out again without having to steal
a separate getaway-vehicle. Ordinary customers still prefer to
walk in and out through the doors in the old-fashioned way.

**Drop-out** A student who fails to complete his education, either at
school or university and adopts an ALTERNATIVE life style. Dropping
in, on the other hand, means to visit someone unexpectedly – or
dropping by in American – but 'dropping someone in it' ('it'
being some sort of trouble or disadvantage) is one of those curious
expressions which are acceptable in polite English conversation
in an abbreviated form, in spite of the fact that everyone knows
that the full version is obscene. See also STOP-OUT.

**Drug abuse** American pseudo-sociological euphemism which
suggests that the *use* of illicit drugs (and hashish is usually implied)
is not harmful, or consoles JUNKIES with the thought that they are
mere social misfits. See also ALCOHOL ABUSE.

# E

**Easy** In its normal sense, not difficult. But as a neologism,
probably inspired by advertising jargon, it appears as 'easy
listening' – a certain type of undemanding, MOR kind of light music;
and wine experts speak of some light wines as 'easy drinking'.

**Editorial** English newspapers have leading-articles, or leaders; American ones are called editorials. *The Times* used to have four leaders, the last of which, known as the Fourth Leader, was always a light-hearted essay. There are now generally only three leaders in this paper, but if one of them is a light essay it is headed 'Fourth Leader'.

**Effete** Now often used as if it were a synonym of 'effeminate', which it is not, although the female sex is relevant to both words. It comes from the Latin *effetus*, meaning 'worn out with child-bearing'. See also EMERITUS.

**Effing and blinding** Euphemism for swearing. The first stands for 'f***ing', the second for 'bloody'.

**Elements** Police jargon for people, as in 'Certain unruly elements . . .' See CHARACTER.

**Elitism** A term of abuse aimed from the LEFT to the RIGHT at those who believe in bettering themselves, the upwardly-mobile and others with professional or educational ambitions. This is nothing more than a belief in the DIFFERENTIAL.

**Embalm** Balm is a contraction of balsam (from French *baume*) – anything that soothes, aromatically improves or preserves, hence

" What is this delicious perfume. my cousin ? You are embalmed like a nosegay ! "

" It is the fashionable, the sweet, and fine perfume which

# VAISSIER'S
# CONGO SOAP,

the most delicate of toilet soaps, leaves behind it on the skin, and on the clothes."

Branch Office for Great Britain and the Colonies;

## C. SIMEONS, & Co.,
70, Finsbury Pavement, London, E.C.

To be had of all Chemists, Perfumers, etc., etc., at 8d., 1s. 3d., and 2s. per cake.

*From The Illustrated London News*

embalming, now exclusively associated with the preservation of dead bodies. But a century ago the word could also be used to denote a fragrance such as a lady might apply to herself.

**Emergent** As in emergent nations, a euphemism for what were at one time called backward or underdeveloped nations; then developing – and now emergent.

**Emeritus** A title given to – most commonly – retired university professors whose wisdom and services are retained in a kind of CONSULTANT (and honorary) capacity. But it is also awarded in other fields, e.g. to orchestral conductors, as a kind of signal meaning that their artistry is now perhaps less highly valued than it used to be. The word comes from the Latin word meaning 'having done good service, old', but definitions vary. For example, Smith's *Smaller Latin-English Dictionary* gives 'unfit for service, worn out'. See also EFFETE.

**(The) end of an era** Journalistic parrot-phrase that is brought out when an important or influential person dies, when a long-established institution closes or some other event occurs which is by some considered to represent the closing of a chapter in human experience. It seldom *is* the end of an era. All it means is that the journalist using the phrase is temporarily stuck for something better to say.

**Endorsement** Very famous people, especially footballers, tennis-stars and those who are famous for being famous such as TELEVISION PERSONALITIES, may be offered large sums of money for pretending to approve of or use certain saleable articles. Such articles may bear their endorser's name and/or portrait, e.g. on articles of clothing, football-boots or tennis-rackets. Occasionally endorsements go delightfully wrong, as when teetotallers endorse alcoholic drinks or non-smokers cigarettes, and reveal their distaste for their 'favourite' products only after having accepted payment.

**Energetic disassembly** Euphemism for a nuclear explosion – a prime example of the obfuscating PENTAGONISM.

**Energy** And this is a good example of the way politicians and mediamen can bend the meaning of words. Energy used to be (among other related or figurative or transferred meanings) the force or power produced by the burning of gas, coal, etc. Now it is the fuel itself (as in 'energy shortage') which is described as energy.

**Entryism**   See MILITANT.

**Environmental cleaners**   New name for what were formerly roadsweepers and dustmen. See CLEANSING OPERATIVES.

**Environmental health officer**   Grand neologist description of an official who used to work under the perfectly dignified title of Public Health Inspector. See also CLEANSING OPERATIVES and RODENT OPERATORS as well as their cross-references.

**Equal opportunities**   One of the great shibboleths of the WELFARE STATE, and often a thumping great lie. Most local authorities, not only the LOONY ones, and also large companies and corporations, add the reassuring line, 'We are an Equal Opportunities Employer' at the foot of their job advertisements – even when they are looking for a Soprano in the BBC Singers, or when the advertisement states (as they often do), 'Preference will be given to applicants of Black or Ethnic origin'. To make sure that all opportunities are not only equal but that some are more equal, there exists a publicly funded Equal Opportunities Commission. See also TOKE.

**Ergonomists**   People with stopwatches who tell us how long it should take to do certain jobs, from Latin *ergo*, therefore.

**(The) establishment**   The OED Supplement magnificently defines the latest meaning of this word as 'A social group exercising power generally, or within a given field or institution, by virtue of its traditional superiority, and by the use especially of *tacit* understandings and often a common mode of speech, and having as a general interest the maintenance of the status quo'. However, the word already had certain shades of meaning in relation to the Established Church, the Royal Navy and Civil Service establishments, etc. During the 1960s the founding of a jazz and cabaret club in Soho, London, sardonically called

the Establishment Club, helped to lend the word an added
meaning.

**Ethnic**  From a Greek word meaning people. Now used to mean
people of dark skin or Asian appearance, usually those who live
in INNER CITY areas. See also GHETTO.

**Euro-**  The all-purpose prefix that swept the English language
when the European Common Market was born, and has not
abated in spite of the often uncomfortable homophony with the
medical uro- prefix.

**Eventuate**  As in 'this is not likely to eventuate': from the usage
of Americans eager to impress with long words, when they could
say 'happen'. But the OED reassures us: '... although still
regarded as an Americansim ... it has been employed by good
writers in England'.

**Executive**  A general-purpose adjective now relentlessly
flogged in every possible commercial context to denote alleged
fashionable desirability and general up-market smartness. Shops
offer executive briefcases, executive hairbrushes, executive
notepaper, hotels executive suites, estate-agents executive town
and country houses and barbers executive hair-styling. The word
comes from the fad for calling every businessman an executive –
which was soon debased when office-boys became 'junior
executives'. But as a CIA euphemism, 'executive action' means
assassination, i.e. 'execution'. See also PLOUGHMAN'S LUNCH.

**(The) ...... experience**  Sales cliché intended to give products
an air of desirability. Thus a certain motor car is advertised as
'The Ultimate Driving Experience' – inadvertently suggesting that
this will be a motorist's last driving experience. Another car is
described as 'The Jaguar Experience'. A food advertisement
bears the headline 'The Butter Experience', and a series of
concerts of music by or around Beethoven is called 'The
Beethoven Experience' etc. But experiences have also spread
into the publishing world, e.g. with a book entitled *The Language
of the Black Experience*, meaning neither more nor less than the
language of black people. See also WORLD.

**Experimental** One of the most useful words in the vocabulary of CONTEMPORARY art in all its forms, whether piles of bricks arranged in art galleries, people smearing their bodies with paint, carrying planks through the streets or making random rude noises with or without musical instruments, YOU NAME IT – it qualifies for the description of 'experimental art'. It is never stated who is experimenting on whom or with what, but the Arts Council can usually help with a subsidy.

**Explicit** Euphemism for OBSCENE, pornographic, an abbreviated form of 'sexually explicit'. From the Latin past participle of *explicare*, to unfold, spread out, free from wrinkles. See also ADULT.

**Extended family** Sociological jargon for a family wider than the NUCLEAR FAMILY, i.e. grandparents, uncles, aunts, second cousins twice removed, etc.

# F

**Fabulous** The unthinkingly inaccurate, modern way of describing anything the speaker or writer considers very good indeed or BRILLIANT. That which is fabulous strictly does not exist except in fables. But the process of weakening strong words is an ancient one – see also AWFUL and LEGENDARY.

**Facility** One of those all-purpose American words which can be made to enhance euphemisms, e.g. 'State Correctional Facility' for a prison.

**Fact-finding trip** A holiday enjoyed by politicians and local-government officers at the expense of their electors/rate-payers.

**Faction** A portmanteau word devised to describe a book or play which contains elements of both *fact* and fic*tion*. It is often heard by way of excuse for the manner in which many television plays and documentaries distort historical truth. Indeed, the word could equally well be a contraction of *fabrication*. There has, of course, long existed such a word which in its original sense was defined as 'A party in the state or any community or association, always in the opprobrious sense, conveying the imputation of mischievous ends or turbulent or unscrupulous methods; a factious quarrel or intrigue; in Ireland, applied to certain mutually hostile associations among the peasantry'. And that definition taken from the first edition of the OED, needs no updating.

**Fag** One of the commonest causes for merry quips between Englishmen and Americans about mutual misunderstandings. In English PUBLIC SCHOOLS a fag used to be a younger boy officially assigned to an older one in order to perform menial tasks for him (or, as the OED rather ambiguously put it, 'to perform certain services'). The fag was required to show absolute obedience, and although his master was allowed to chastise or otherwise punish him, the avowed purpose of the arrangement was that the senior partner might in this way learn how in later life to treat his servants fairly and responsibly. The system was open to abuse, to some sexual perversion and general exploitation, and has now been all but abolished in English public schools. In the United States, however, the word *fag* is an abbreviation of *faggot* and means a homosexual. There is an anecdote about a British diplomat replying to his American counterpart's question whether he (the British diplomat) had known his ambassador a long time or knew him well. The Briton replied, 'Very well indeed. We were at Eton together. As a matter of fact, I used to fag for him.' The American replied, 'My – you British are nothing if not frank!' In colloquial, non-public-school English, a fag is most commonly either a tiresome, unpleasant chore ('It's a bit of a fag but I'll have to do it'); or a cigarette. In this sense the word was shared with the Americans before *fag(got)* took over ... During the First World War the boys of the American Expeditionary Force used to sing *'Strike up a Lucifer\* and light your fag/And smile, boys, that's the style.'*

**Fan** Allegedly a keen supporter, as in pop-music or sport, but in fact an abbreviation of 'fanatic', and therefore often one who expresses his adherence by violent behaviour – like FUNDAMENTALISTS.

\* Lucifer – the brand-name of a match.

**Farm fresh**  One of a number of product descriptions used in large print by food manufacturers, their fanciful adjectives ranging from the meaningless to the downright fraudulent. For the chemical reality the small type has to be examined, and for examples of both see any food packaging. However, they also often claim that food comes to us 'at the peak of freshnes', which makes one wonder what it will be like a few hours later.

**Featherbedding**  'The action of making comfortable by favourable, especially economic or financial, treatment' – which the British farmer has for many decades enjoyed as an almost traditional right; and his bed became even more comfortable with the help of EURO-subsidies. Now, however, a colder wind is blowing from Europe and the production of food that swells the INTERVENTIONist surplus produce may eventually reach more realistic levels. Alliterative cries against 'featherbedding the farmers' have been heard since the 1920s, but the expression was at first also used – less effectively – against the trades unions, especially 'in the employment of superfluous staff' (OED).

**Fellow-traveller**  One who, although not known to be a communist himself, is said to have sympathy with the communist cause. But the expression can, of course, be used derogatorily of other sympathisers with unpopular causes. The OED Supplement traces the first political use of the term to the American magazine *The Nation*, in 1936: 'The new phenomenon is the fellow-traveler. The term has a Russian background and means someone who does not accept all your aims but has enough in common with you to accompany you in a comradely fashion part of the way'. The Russian background is owed to Leon Trotsky, who used the word *popuchik* – see also the -NIK suffix which gave us the sputnik, meaning fellow-traveller, i.e. satellite.

**Fest**  The German word for festival adopted into American as a facetious suffix, e.g. gab-fest for an occasion such as a conference where there is much talking, food-fest, love-fest and even, in the generation-long American feast of permissiveness whose chickens are now coming home to roost – the f*ck-fest. Conservative Party conferences have been described as 'Thatcherfests'.

**(The) fifth man** We speak of the THIRD WORLD but seldom of the first and second; similarly there is a Fifth Man in British spy lore. The first, second, third and fourth men, Guy Burgess, Donald Maclean, Kim Philby and Anthony Blunt, respectively, were all working as Soviet spies or agents for Bolshevik Russia (see BOLSHY) while at the same time active members of the British Secret Service. According to popular belief there was another spy who was prominent in public life but whose identity is said to have been suppressed. The guessing-game Naming The Fifth Man has kept a number of British journalists in business for decades. Such numberings come easily to the British, probably because 'men' are counted in cricket according to their batting-order – including the Twelfth Man and indeed the Nightwatchman.

**Fighter** A euphemism favoured by JOURNOS, especially those working for the BBC and COMMERCIAL news, when they should say TERRORIST but are, for one reason or another, reluctant to take sides. Thus they hedge their bets and with mistaken evenhandedness describe evil men as neutral 'fighters' instead of saying 'Shite Amal Terrorists' ('Shi'ite' is another nervous modification to avoid misunderstandings). Where the IRA and its Protestant Ulster terrorist counterparts are concerned no such compunction is shown. However, here the MEDIA unquestioningly parrot the ludicrous names, ranks and titles these ideological brigands award themselves, using words like 'Chief-of-Staff' or 'Quartermaster-General' to describe paramilitary youths barely out of their teens. See also FREEDOM FIGHTER.

**(The) .... File** Pretentious title cliché, often used in order to lend a touch of sensationalism to newspaper articles written by INVESTIGATIVE JOURNALISTS.

**First world** See THIRD WORLD.

**Flavour of the month/week/year** Something enjoying a remarkable but probably temporary popularity. Perhaps derived from American-Italian ice-cream parlours.

**Fleet Street** A synecdochal, figurative term for the London-based press, although many important newspapers have for various reasons moved away from the street OF SHAME. Fleet-street (as it

was usually written until 20th century JOURNOS all but abolished
hyphens) is named after the River Fleet, an evil-smelling open
sewer which ran between Ludgate Hill and Fleet Street until
covered over in the 19th century – the first of many Fleet Street
cover-ups. The word *fleet* has many meanings, says the OED,
including 'evanescent, shifting, not durable or lasting', and 'that
which floats upon the surface of a liquid', i.e. scum.

**Flexible friend** A credit card. From a television advertisement.
Such cards now 'do nicely' – from another television advertisment.
Thus are our clichés manufactured. See also PLASTIC.

**Floor** 'The floor', without further qualification, has many
meanings according to context. In industry it means the shop-
floor, where the actual work is done and the shop-stewards wield
power, but on the shop-floors of the HIGH STREET the fast-
disappearing shopwalker is in charge; in political and trades
union meetings, the floor comprises the participating audience
from the GRASS ROOTS ('There were noisy contributions from the
floor . . .'.); and in football, 'the floor' really *is* made of grass –
because sportsmen and their commentators fail to distinguish
between 'the floor' and 'the ground'. In television it means the
areas where the cameras and the performers operate under
instructions from the floor manager. Among other neologist floors
are those in wages, etc., which – not unnaturally – are at the
opposite end of the equally figurative ceilings. See also GAFFER.

**Flying pickets** See RENT-A-

**Fogey** Old fogeys have long been with us – staid, respectable,
middle-class persons (of either sex though more often male) who
are set in their ways and conservative (probably also
Conservative) in outlook. Now, with increasing stress laid on
material success among younger people, the Young Fogeys are
with us. They are staid, respectable, middle-class, conservative
and almost certainly Conservative, and under the age of thirty.
They have YUPPIE leanings and read the *Times*, the *Spectator*,
*Private Eye* or the *Independent* rather than the *Guardian*, the
*Listener* or the TABLOIDS, are found in greater concentration in
London than the REGIONS and are more likely to work in finance
than industry.

**Foodie** One who is inordinately devoted to the pleasures of eating; or indeed one who is addicted to food, as the word is an adaptation of JUNKIE. The invention of the word has been claimed by Ann Barr and Paul Levy (Letter to the *Times*, 20th April 1987) with the title of their *Official Foodie Handbook* (1984).

**Footman** In its older sense, a servant, presumably one who 'waits hand and foot', the male equivalent of a handmaiden (but see also AMANUENSIS); now, police slang for one of their men on the beat, as opposed to those who ride in patrol cars or on motor-cycles. See also LEG MAN and STRINGER.

**Foreigner** 'Doing a foreigner' is a manifestation of the BLACK economy: one of many ways of 'beating the SYSTEM'. It is a form of private enterprise and means undertaking outside work on a freelance basis without one's employer's knowledge. If it is done in the employer's time and carried out with materials stolen from him, then the triumph is complete. Of income-tax and VAT it is unnecessary to speak.

**Forename** Surely to be preferred – like First Name or Given Name – to 'Christian Name', especially on official forms or when a person's religion is not known. Thomas, James, Mary and Joseph are Christian names; Tudor, Leslie, Stanley, Tracy, Wendy and the rest are not; and Moses, Ruth, Abraham, Rachel, Ahmed and Abdulla certainly not.

**Fornicatorium** Popular name for a motor-car used for amatory purposes, pioneered in the United States, where young couples used to go to DRIVE-IN cinemas and apparently enjoy films through the steamed-up windows of their cars. It was said that before the advent of the permissive society and television (which between them all but ruined the drive-in cinema) more American children were conceived in cars than in beds. See also DIRTY MAC BRIGADE.

**Forte** The Italian word for strong – not loud, although in music it often comes to the same thing. Unlike the curious misuse of CRESCENDO it is therefore perfectly accurate to speak of 'someone's forte', though again 'strength' is just as good, and English.

**Fratting** Post-war British forces' slang word, an abbreviation of 'fraternising with the enemy', an activity forbidden to British occupying troops. In practice 'fraternising' meant GOING OUT WITH and/or sleeping with German women; and purists held that it should really have been 'sororising'.

**Freebie** Anything received, consumed or enjoyed without cost to the receiver, usually by journalists (who are great freeloaders and receivers of PERKS) i.e. a FACILITY trip, a party given by publishers, industrial firms or embassies, or 'promotional material' given away free to those thought by the givers to be able to publicise them or their products. Travel writers and motoring correspondents traditionally get the most spectacular freebies abroad. But as there is no such thing as a free lunch so there are no free freebies. The customer always pays. The OED dates the first known appearance of the word as 1942. Companies as well as countries receive alleged freebies from newspapers, in the form of SPECIAL REPORTS. See also TWINNING.

**Freedom fighter** See TERRORIST.

**Free-sheet** A newspaper which is given away free, usually in the form of JUNK mail, and which derives its revenue from advertising. This depends on published circulation figures, and in such quasi-newspapers there are none, as there is no guarantee that house-to-house distributors actually distribute them. In many an INNER CITY area whole bundles of free-sheets may be found abandoned on rubbish-dumps by delivery-boys who like to get home early – the numbers duly included in circulation figures.

**French** The word seems to be losing its 'saucy' associations – French knickers, French kissing, French postcards, French novels ('My scrofulous French novel/ On grey paper with blunt type', as Robert Browning's soliloquising monk says in a Spanish Cloister); and, of course, French letters (see CONDOM). For a Frenchman's lunch see under PLOUGHMAN'S LUNCH.

**Fresh** Clean, fragrantly new, newly-picked (of fruit), newly baked (e.g. bread), full of vigour, not tired or exhausted, etc., etc. But in modern (especially radio news) usage it is an over-employed and not very apt synonym for 'renewed', as in fresh fighting, fresh talks, fresh wage increases – when no freshness is indicated. Also, as in 'Don't you get fresh with me!', a HOBSON-JOBSON Americanism adapted from the sound and meaning of the German word *frech*, cheeky, impertinent.

**Friendly neighbourhood-** Prefix words originating in American commercial jargon – 'Your friendly neighbourhood store', etc. but now satirised bathetically into such formations as 'Your friendly neighbourhood' rapist, burglar, planner, developer... etc.

**Frontlash** See BACKLASH.

**Front line states** The countries surrounding the South African Republic and, most of them, overtly hostile to it, although some are by necessity on good terms with the enemy as they depend on South African import, export and transport facilities. See also HOME COUNTIES.

**Fruitist** An *ism* word which never entered British English but had a brief vogue in the United States, where traditional free enterprise and unrestrained commerce have always spawned imaginative (and some extremely ugly) names for shops, companies and their entreprises – see -AMA, -TERIA, -ORIUM, etc. Farmer's *Dictionary of Americanisms* in 1889 wrote: 'FRUITIST, a cultivator of fruit trees. One of a class of words in *ist*, some few of which are useful, but which in the main are hideous monstrosities. What in the world can be said for such forms as "walkist", "shootist", "singist", "landscapist", and, oh Minerva! "obituarist"'. Farmer would be interested to know that today, almost a century later, only the last two are in anything like general use.

**FU** An ambiguous abbreviation. In normal use it is short for the imprecation 'F... you!', but among society women anxious for their daughters to meet and marry rich young men, FU stands for 'financially unsuitable'.

**Fubar** See SNAFU.

**Fubb** See SNAFU.

**Fubis** See SNAFU.

**Fumtu** See SNAFU.

**Fundamentalists** Religious fanatics (see FAN). The original word comes from America, where the first fundamentalists were Protestants who in the early 1920s founded a sect that believed in the strictest possible and literal adherence to the fundamental tenets of the Christian faith. Not an idea that would cause much harm to outsiders, but since the spectacular rise of Islamic politico-religious fanaticism from the 1970s (as exemplified by the Iranian revolution) fundamentalists have more often been Arabs. Their activities range from self-flagellation (and, more rarely, self-immolation) to the killing of innocents. Which, in a way, is reminiscent of early Christian practices.

# G

**Gaffer** 'A term applied originally by country people to an elderly man or one whose position entitles him to respect' – in other words a way of addressing a boss or other man of superior professional position, e.g. the foreman of a gang of workers. In Hollywood movie slang – and hence British television – a gaffer is the chief electrician on the set or FLOOR. The word is now very familiar from the credits of TV programmes, as the lengthy titles roll up, down or across the screen at great speed, giving credit to every participant of the enterprise. Gaffer is a rustic (possibly also juvenile) contraction of 'grandfather'. Perhaps the already vastly overmanned television and film industry might find room for a few tea-ladies and call them 'gammers' – the related abbreviation of 'grandmothers'. Another kind of electrical artisans get credits as 'grips'.

**Gallery** A pretentious name for a shop, and a place where goods sold are described as COLLECTIONS. Probably derived from the name of a famous French shop, *Galeries Lafayette*. See also -RAMA, -ORIUM and their various cross-references.

**Garden flat** Estate agents' jargon for a basement. Others include 'In need of modernisation' = derelict; '. . . of character' = old and derelict; 'picturesque' = old, derelict and probably remote; '. . . of traditional design' = old but not period; 'compact' = small; 'bijou' = small and pokey; 'labour-saving kitchen' = one so small that you can do everything while standing in one spot; 'mature garden' = full of weeds and overgrown; 'shrubs' = a privet hedge; 'close to bus route' = on a busy main road; 'close to motorway' = under a spaghetti junction; 'car space' = concrete front yard, etc.

**Genteelism** Defined by Fowler in 1926 as '. . . the substituting, for the ordinary natural word that first suggests itself to the mind, of a synonym that is thought to be less soiled by the lips of the common herd, less familiar, less plebeian, less vulgar, less improper'.

**Gentrification** The process by which houses and flats in urban (more rarely, rural) areas occupied by poorer people are gradually taken over by richer occupants, usually from the YUPPIE or professional classes. The term is considered opprobrious and is often heard from LEFTists when abusing their opponents. It is seldom used by estate agents, who encourage the process without appearing to admit it.

**George Spelvin** See WALTER PLINGE and JOHN DOE.

**Ghetto** In 1516 Venice had a ghetto to which Jews were confined, partly for their own safety against attack by zealous Christians and partly so that their teachings would not threaten those of the established religion. It was built on the site of an iron-foundry, the word for which is *getto* in Italian; and that is how the name is thought by some to have come about. Today's ghettos are no longer Jewish, nor are they enclosed by walls and gates but are run-down INNER CITY areas occupied largely by poorer people of ETHNIC origin.

**Ghost** A spectre or supernatural being, invisible to all but those who believe in such manifestations. The evenhanded OED also admits 'ghostess – a female ghost'. In a more tangible (though no less invisible) everyday sense, ghosts write books, articles, scripts, jokes or speeches for those who wish to pass them off as

their own work. By their very nature, such ghosts must remain in
the background or they defeat their purpose, preferring fees to
fame. Much more ghosting goes on in the world of the written
and spoken word than most people realise. In politics, few public
figures write their own speeches but employ speech-writers to
compose them on their behalf. Most of the memorable political
(and a few royal) sayings that find their way into books like this
one were put into celebrated mouths. Nearly all successful
politicians, some of whom have won prizes and acclaim for their
alleged journalistic efforts, employ a veritable army of assistants
to do the actual work, although these may be provided with ideas
and outlines. Even as great a master of the English language as
Winston Churchill did not write his many historical volumes
unaided. As a prominent and busily active politician and
statesman, when would he have found the time to do so, just to
have written down the words, let alone composed them? After his
death, when his son Randolph, also a politician (though an
ineffectual one), followed in his father's footsteps as a writer, a
newspaper photograph appeared, captioned, 'Mr Randolph
Churchill at work writing his father's biography' – but showing a
room the size of a small aeroplane-hangar, desk beyond desk,
stretching into the distance, each manned by a ghost and a
typewriter. The same goes for many a fat volume of political
theory produced by politicians, though their memoirs and diaries
might be typed and edited versions of tape-recorded aides-
memoire, which many conscientiously speak into their dictating-
machines each night. Another euphemism for ghosts is
RESEARCHERS, but these are now more associated with television. In
the WORLD of fiction, many BLOCKBUSTERS by world-famous authors
are the work of many hands. In some instances the author devises
the – often highly ingenious – plots and hands over the outline of
the book to the publishers, whose editors, perhaps with a small
group of hired writers, produce the version the public buys and
the critics may praise. After the dying Mozart had received that
famous visit from a mysterious, spectral figure, the 'Man in Grey',
who asked him to write a Requiem, Mozart said he believed the
messenger was a ghost. But the man was real enough. He merely
came on behalf of a Count Walsegg who was in the habit of buying
compositions from famous composers and passing them off as his
own; so that he was expecting Mozart to act as ghost. See also AS
TOLD TO ..., PACKAGING and RESEARCHER.

**Girl Friday** A kind of female AMANUENSIS (or handmaiden) modified from Man Friday, Robinson Crusoe's helper on his desert island. Advertisements for Girls Friday (or Girl Fridays – the plural varies) are now illegal unless the job description is neutered as 'PERSON Friday'. See also CHAIR.

**Girlie** Formerly an affectionate term for a young or diminutive girl. Now it means a girl without any clothes on, perhaps appearing in a Girlie Magazine or on PAGE THREE of a TABLOID and, in respect of her VITAL STATISTICS, not at all diminutive.

**Girl talk** The conversation among women when men are not present – the topics being usually men, love, sex, clothes, and all the other various ills – real or imagined – of the female condition. In this sense 'girls' can be of any age, as in 'girlfriend'; though men are 'boys' less readily, except when they are 'all boys together'. Then, in pubs, clubs or offices, the men boast about cars, women, sex and income (see K), but talk little of love and hardly at all of their ailments, of which they are not proud and which are usually confined to piles, ruptures, alcoholism and heart-attacks. All this, however, is not called 'boy talk' though, like their female counterparts, they can be 'boyfriends' well into and beyond old age, especially when their amatory activities are reported in newspapers.

**Glasnost** A Russian word which has swept across the world since the beginning of 1987, when it came like a breath of spring, both in Russia and the West. It is generally translated as 'openness', but comes from the adjective *glasnyi,* 'open to public information and discussion' – in other words, a welcome sign of the new order brought into force by Mikhail Gorbachev – a totally new order, incidentally, never previously enjoyed by Russians, either during the reign of the 'terrorist' czars (see Foreword) or the COMMISSARS. Long may it last. Perhaps in time even the GULAGS and PSYCHIATRIC HOSPITALS will be thrown open to release DISSIDENTS and REFUSENIKS, so that these words, too, may become part of history.

**Global** As in global view, global concept, global VILLAGE, etc. A word used chiefly by boasters and idealists, suggesting totality or world-wide universality. There is also the related *ism,* globalism, which is the opposite of isolationism. Some people happily speak of 'The four corners of the globe'. See also WORLD.

**Glossies** These are magazines which, unlike the PULPS, are printed on shiny, i.e. coated, paper – mostly in order to make the advertisements look more alluring. In every other way most of them are just as ephemeral.

**Going out with** In lower-middle and working-class usage, GIRL-TALK euphemism for sleeping (i.e. having sexual intercourse) with someone. It comes from the much older, rustic-biblical English euphemism 'going with' ('And the ram went with the ewe.').

**Good in parts** See (LIKE THE) CURATE'S EGG.

**-gram** When the British Post Office monopoly all but abolished the internal telegram and replaced it with an overnight(!) letter called the 'Telemessage', it presented an opportunity for entrepreneurs to fill the gap in the greetings trade. At first they showed some originality, but soon the idea suffered much extension-by-imitation. All manner of messenger-borne greetings have become available – from kissograms and gorillagrams to strippagrams, nursograms, etc. Also singing telegrams, which generally involve the tuneless singing of a message, to the great embarrassment of all concerned. In fact the chief value of the service seems to be not so much to greet the recipient as to cause him as much embarrassment as possible, and maximum hilarity to bystanders. Many claims have been laid to the invention of the idea (at any rate in England). Those who do so should consult Farmer's *Dictionary of Americanisms Old and New* (1889), where they will read: 'Happygram: A spurious word, partially moulded on a much-discussed pattern, i.e. "telegram" . . .'. (And note that 'telegram' was then still much discussed, though it soon became accepted as a standard, everyday word, often replaced by 'cable', which is an anachronism now that most telegraphy works by wireless or even satellite.)

**Grand** Originally American slang – probably first used by gangsters and other shady dealers as a kind of code – for a thousand dollars. Now also a thousand pounds when said by

Britons, especially those who are reticent or shy when talking about money and are glad for any euphemism, e.g. 'lolly', 'the dibs', 'the wherewithal', 'the ready', etc. See also K.

**Grass roots** In political applications, which is where grass roots (grass-roots or grassroots) are most commonly found, this means the rank and file of a political movement, or the majority of its supposed supporters, where there may be found a GROUNDSWELL of opinion. What is needed to get rid of too many sprouting grass roots is a good dose of selective word-killer.

**Grim** In media language, and when coupled with 'task', this invariably means the recovery or examination of corpses. No other adjective will do, nor apparently is 'task' on its own considered strong enough.

**Groundswell** From this imaginary manifestation politicians claim to be able to find out what the CLIMATE OF OPINION is among the GRASS ROOTS – perhaps those protected by an UMBRELLA organisation. A groundswell was originally a maritime phenomenon well known to sailors, who could detect a distant storm or even an earthquake by studying certain, often though not necessarily quite gentle, agitations on the surface of the sea. Coleridge is thought to have been the first to apply this figuratively, in 1817, when he wrote of 'the ground-swell of a teeming instinct'.

**Gulag** Russian acronym now usually taken to denote a Soviet labour or concentration camp (see also PSYCHIATRIC HOSPITAL). *Gulag* is constructed from three words, G (*osudarstvennoye*) U (*pravleniye*) and LAG (*erey*), meaning, literally, 'State Directorate of the Camps'. It is therefore acronymically related to the Nazi prisoner-of-war camps of evil memory in the Second World War, *Oflag* and *Stalag,* whose final elements are abbreviated from *Lager*, which meant a camp long before it suggested the gaseous continental LAGER beer.

# H

**Hacks** See JOURNOS.

**Haigisms** Probably more commonly called 'Haigspeak'; see under PENTAGONISMS.

**Hamlet** See VILLAGE.

**Hand-crafted** Jargon of small-time commerce meaning 'hand-made' but with the intended (but often unwarranted) suggestion of traditional craftsmanship.

**Handicapped** One of a large number of kindly-meant euphemisms, like DISABLED, devised in order that people who are in some way infirm or crippled might feel less bad about their affliction. 'Mentally handicapped', which embraces all kinds and degrees of illnesses of the mind is, however, to be preferred to the old-fashioned and far too all-embracing 'mad'; though it is often misunderstood to the detriment of the sufferer. Had the person who first applied the word 'handicap' in this way known that it comes from the expression 'hand in the cap', he or she would doubtless have chosen a different one.

**Handling** One of the many SPANISH CUSTOMS traditionally engaged in by British workers as well as industry and commerce and described under that heading. Unsuspecting customers may also find that when they received payment-demands for goods they have bought, a 'Handling Charge' has been added, when it would seem only to be expected that goods bought and sold would have to be 'handled' in some way by the seller. 'Refusal to Handle' is one of the mainstays of British INDUSTRIAL ACTION, and can be applied to goods or other items that do *not* need to be handled.

**Hardhat** A construction-worker. From the plastic safety-helmet worn by these persons. The colour of the hat may denote rank, hence also 'whitehat', 'yellowhat', etc.

**Hardliners and softliners** A curious Americanism from political news usage which to the British eye and ear is uncomfortably close to words like binliners. See HAWKS AND DOVES and WETS; also SOFT LEFT, and MILITANT, and various other cross-referenced shades and hues of British politics; and the Colour Supplement at the end of this book.

**Harmonisation** This has nothing to do with music or singing together but is EURO-jargon for squabbling among member-states in order that one or another might obtain the greatest advantage at the expense of the rest. The real meaning is usually that prices are raised.

**Hash** American word (through survival of older English usage) for minced meat – which is not to be confused with the English mincemeat, a mixture of dried fruit and fruit-peel, nor with the common abbreviation for hashish.

**Hassle** Any kind of bother, difficulty, argument, disagreement, or an unpleasant rush: of mid-20th-century American origin but since the 1960s considered a normal, useful and respectable English colloquialism – and one which (doubtless because of its sibilant force) has found much favour in some circles. In Wentworth & Flexner is given a 1947 usage in a different spelling: 'A hassel between two actors ...' and *Webster's New Collegiate Dictionary* (1951) suggests a portmanteau formation from *haggle* and *tussle,* though a relationship with the German word for hate, *hassen,* seems more plausible.

**Having it good** Harold Macmillan, later the first Earl of Stockton (1894–1986), was probably the last of the great cultured English statesmen, perhaps first a well-educated, highly literate gentleman and only by chance a politician. In spite of this, he departed from his customary standards of grammar in two of his three best-known sayings, one an Americanism and the other a Cockney double-negative. Speaking at a Conservative Party Rally in 1957 he said, 'Let us be frank about it, most of our people have never had it so good'; and, at a press conference on his return from a summit conference in 1955, 'There ain't gonna be no war.' The third was the famous 'wind of change' speech in South Africa.

**Hawks and doves** The hawk is a bird of prey, whereas the dove has been a symbol of love, gentleness and peace ever since one perched on the arm of Aphrodite, and another told Noah that God had pacified the waters of the Flood. Political hawks are bellicosely aggressive politicians and statesmen, and were originally called 'War Hawks' – the term coined in 1798 by Thomas Jefferson, who so described those of his fellow-Americans who wanted to wage war on France. This was later occasionally modified to 'War Dogs' (doubtless with reference to Shakespeare's DOGS OF WAR). As William Safire points out (in *The New Language of Politics*, 1968), 'Some will find comfort in the fact that the American bald eagle is a species of hawk; others will point out that its close relation is the vulture.' See also British WETS and dries, HARD-LINERS AND SOFT-LINERS, etc.

**Head-hunting** The process of persuading successful senior EXECUTIVES, e.g. existing or potential *heads* of departments, in commerce and industry, to leave their jobs and take up better-paid ones in rival companies. It is more a process of poaching than head-hunting, and the practice has its roots in the rather ruthless, aggressive way American business works. Wentworth & Flexner define a head-hunter as 'the owner or boss of an executive employment agency; a business executive in charge of recruiting new personnel'. There are agencies whose main activities lie in this specialised field, and their advertisements are full of specialised terms, e.g. HIGH-FLYERS and SELF-STARTERS.

**Heath Robinson** As in 'a Heath Robinson contraption': said of a makeshift device or invention – usually one that works in spite of being roughly constructed or improvised. From the name of a British artist, W. Heath Robinson (1872–1944), who was famous for his cartoons about mad inventors and their strange devices.

**Heterosexism** Alleged discrimination in favour of people who are not homosexual. See also the various cross-referenced LOONY entries and the introduction.

**High-flyers** Successful young business EXECUTIVES or YUPPIES, young FOGEYS, or perhaps even DINKIES – probably the sort that are the object of HEAD-HUNTING. High-flyers observe certain conventions of dress, e.g. the wearing of striped shirts (though not with broad stripes, which are the preserve of politicians) and indulge in the apparently compulsive removal of jackets whenever they enter a room. This is intended to be an outward signal of their willingness to work hard. I recently sat in the underheated dining-room of a Scottish hotel known for its CONFERENCE facilities and watched as scores of freshly groomed young executives (all taking part in the same SEMINAR) came down

---

**FRENCH**
French speaking P.A./Secretary with floorless English,
good English shorthand and word processing/personal
computer experience, required by City merchant bank. We

---

*Head-hunting for a high-flying executive?*

for breakfast. Each one, without exception, removed his jacket
and hung it over the back of his chair before sitting down to eat
his 'Full English(!) breakfast'. The air was thick with aftershave
and deodorant (but not cigarette-smoke, for the true high-flyer,
YUPPIE or young FOGEY abhors this dangerous habit). High-flying
orchestral conductors, on the other hand, who have more reason
than businessmen for removing garments as they engage in often
strenuous exercise, follow their own professional custom of (when
not actually conducting) draping their jacket loosely over the
shoulder, sleeves dangling empty. High-flyers are always SELF-
STARTERS and imbued with MOTIVATION. In their spare time they may
be HOORAY HENRYS or even SLOANE RANGERS.

**High street** A usually imaginary place where according to
newspaper and radio JOURNOS the 'high-street bank' and 'high-
street building-societies' have their premises. See also CORNER
SHOPS.

**Hobson-Jobson** The manner of adopting a foreign word to its
nearest English sound and making from it an English word or
words. Thus the Spanish exclamation *O mihi beate Martini!* is said
to have been adapted by British sailors to 'All my eye and Betty
Martin!' Hobson-Jobson itself is an adaptation of the cry *Ya Hasan
Ya Husayn!* heard by British troops in Muslim countries. Also
reported as *Hosseen Gosseen!* and *Hossein Yossen!* etc. There is
a splendid dictionary, *Hobson-Jobson*, by Yule and Burnell, first
published in 1886 and reprinted in 1985 by Routledge.

**-holic** From the Greek-based word alcoholic (when used as a noun, meaning someone addicted to alcohol). The ending is often adapted to make words facetiously suggesting addiction, e.g. foodaholic (see also FOODIE), workaholic, bookaholic, etc. See also -OCRACY.

**Holistic** See WHOLE.

**Holocaust** The Greek/Latin-based word for 'burn everything' (*holos* meaning whole and *kaustos,* burn), a word which has always been associated with sacrifice and martyrdom. It is now often applied to the wartime murder of millions of Jews by the Nazi Germans, and was in this sense first used in a book by the writer Elie Wiesel, a Nobel prizewinner in 1986.

**Home Counties** The counties which immediately surround London – a term which reveals the arrogance of the prosperous south versus the poorer north, now called the North–South Divide – a term which identifies undoubted wrongs but does nothing to alleviate them. See also FRONT LINE STATES.

**Home economics** A school subject which started as the homely Housekeeping (or Cookery) Class but graduated to this more impressive title, via Domestic Science. What is often behind such renamings is a desire to appease those who relentlessly pursue SEX TYPING.

**Home help** One of the many examples of the need Britons appear to feel for avoiding plain, factual descriptions of ways of serving or helping each other, and clothing them in euphemisms. Few of those who can afford to employ servants admit the fact other than by circumlocution, e.g. 'my daily [!] who comes and does for me once a week'. The home help is one of these; but it is also a term employed by the WELFARE STATE, which sends persons to help others who are unable to help themselves, one of the many admirable manifestations of the caring society. But why not 'helper'? Help is what the helper brings. For another kind of euphemistic servant, see GIRL FRIDAY.

**Homophobic** Originally, fearing man, e.g. like a nervous animal that flees. Now, in the LOONY leftspeak, the meaning has been bent to mean discrimination against homosexuals. As a Mr Russell Profitt, described by his employers as 'Principal Race Relations Advisor [sic!] to Brent Borough Council', said, 'The local Tories … are using a homophobic argument against some of the council's policies, particularly about gay and lesbian rights.' The change is particularly foolish as *homo,* the Latin word for man both in the sense of mankind and as the opposite of woman, is denied validity by some men-hating lesbian feminists and WIMMIN.

**Hong Kong dog** See AZTEC TWO-STEP.

**Hooker** American word for a prostitute which gained currency in Britain after the showing of a film with that title. Previously it meant an angler, and, by extension, a thief who fished for property. (See also PUNTER.)

**Hooray Henrys** (Sometimes written 'Hurrah' and/or 'Henries'): A member of the upper (or YUPPIE) classes who is usually though not always male and behaves badly and rowdily in the company of others of his kind. On his own the Hooray Henry is harmless, well-behaved and probably even kind to old people. He always belongs to, or at least is always presumed to support, the Conservative Party. Young FOGEYS strongly disapprove of Hooray Henrys/Henries. For an historical precedent, see under BLOODY.

**Horse trials** See KANGAROO COURTS.

**How's your father** Not a question but a kind of all-purpose euphemism or expletive (in the proper sense of that word, i.e. a filling-in). Thus a doctor asking a patient intimate questions while wishing to avoid using both crudely colloquial and obscurely medical words, might say to him, 'And does the old how's-your-father still work all right?' The phrase probably originated in the English music-hall, when a comedian telling a BLUE joke would break off at the point when his innuendo becomes clear to the audience and ask, 'By the way, how's your father?' See also NUDGE-NUDGE, WINK-WINK.

**Human chain** Three or more people linking hands, as described by newsmen or by the participants if the action takes place for publicity purposes.

**Human torch** News cliché for a person whose clothes have caught fire, however slightly.

# I

**Ice-pick socialism** A facetious name for the factional in-fighting among proponents of different kinds of LEFT-wing extremism. Such extremists, frequently referred to here and elsewhere as LOONIES, are not always as lunatic as they like us to believe they are but aim at DESTABILISING Western society. They adhere to a multitude of *isms* too numerous (and often too silly) to describe in this book; and in their quest for revolution are prepared even to bloody each other's heads in support of these beliefs. 'Trots' (who are also subdivided into many and various factional hues) can never forgive Stalinists that Leon Trotsky (né 1879 Leon Davidovich Bronstein) was factionally murdered in 1940 in Mexico City by one of Stalin's hit-men – and that at a time when Stalin should have spent his energies fighting Nazism.

**If-you-like** A common but meaningless phrase used in informal, impromptu speech, e.g. in discussions if-you-like and interviews. This interjection if-you-like is interspersed at random in sentences as a kind of expletive if-you-like, possibly to show hesitancy if-you-like on the part of the speaker. The apparent intention appears to be if-you-like that the listener is given a choice if-you-like but that is not the case. I, for one, do not like, but it is nothing more than a sort of nervous speech-tic. The less articulate have long used -like as a suffix-like, when they are not certain-like what they mean-like. If-you-like is only an upmarket version of that. Older people add the occasional involuntary 'sort-of' or 'kind-of'. I sometimes do. But not the older still 'don'tcherknow'.

**I'm sorry?** Colloquial abbreviation of 'I'm sorry, I didn't hear/understand what you said', often further abbreviated to 'sorry?', and both spoken with a questioning inflexion. Various English conventions come into play and have given rise to these expressions. It is, for example, considered non-u to say 'pardon?' (and worse to make it sound phoney-French by stressing it on the second syllable, 'par*dong*?'), but socially acceptable to put it

in full: 'I beg your pardon?' Also, 'What?', the almost peremptory
invitation to repeat what has been said but not said loudly or
clearly enough, is considered rude only by those who would
prefer 'par-*dong*?' No YUPPIE would ever commit such solecisms.

**In-** A prefix of commerce, of the modern materialist society and
its conspicuous consumption. Firms offer not car radios but 'in-
car entertainment', do their own 'in-house printing' and 'in-plant
typesetting'. Other prepositional off-beat changes include terms
like 'on-train catering', with 'at-table' service.

**-in** The -in suffix became fashionable in the 1960s, after some
courageous negroes (often accompanied by sympathetic whites)
in the American southern states entered and sat down in
restaurants from which negroes were excluded. The sit-in was,
however, named after the jazz practice of 'sitting-in'. This occurs
when an additional or guest player temporarily joins an
established band, and this eventually led to love-ins, work-ins,
teach-ins, etc., the last-named chiefly at the trendier universities,
where the word supplanted what more traditionally-minded
establishments in their stuffy and boring way continued to call
lectures.

**Incursion** American PENTAGONESE euphemism for an invasion,
generally one approved of, or supported by, the Americans
themselves.

**Independent television/radio** Euphemism for COMMERCIAL
TELEVISION/radio.

**Industrial action** Strikers' euphemism for a strike. Often
shortened to 'action', which is ludicrous, since action then means
inaction. Teachers also take industrial action, although they would
hotly deny that teaching was an industry.

**Info** An increasingly common abbreviation ('abbro'?) of
'information'. Probably from the armed services, e.g.
ammo = ammunition. See also -O.

**Inner city** This absurd term is now absurdly used to mean
nothing more nor less than a run-down urban area, even when it

is five miles from the 'inner' area of the city in question. It is in such areas that GHETTOS are situated, where HAMLETS are often occupied by the poor in general and by people of ETHNIC origin in particular.

**Innocent bystander** Self-description for a demonstrator or rioter who suffers injury.

**.... in residence** Writers, Poets, Painters and others may be offered, if they are lucky, a paid attachment to some institution – anything from an orchestra to a prison, whose inmates are meant to benefit from their proximity and watch them work. It is a form of public recognition as well as patronage, and such artists may then describe themselves as Writers (or whatever) in Residence. The cash is usually provided by the public (i.e. the Arts Council or local government). Some say this is a good method of giving money to deserving or struggling people; others, that it is yet another way of wasting funds. The 'residence' part is, however, not meant to be taken seriously, as artists are expected to return to their garrets each night; and in any case seldom spend much time with those they are meant to inspire. In 1986 Manchester Polytechnic appointed a Basketmaker-in-Residence.

**Insider dealing** A specialist financial term which, like BIG BANG, entered general usage during the middle 1980s. It means taking advantage of 'inside' knowledge not available to the investing public in order to gain an advantage in the buying and selling of shares. Huge profits may thus be made before anyone else is aware of impending plans, e.g. for take-overs by or of large companies. No-one seems to know how such dealing, which is illegal, can be guarded against, since those with inside knowledge, in whatever field, know more than outsiders and are able to tip off accomplices or nominees. Insider dealing has doubtless played its part in the rise of the YUPPIES and their inordinately high earnings. There is probably another element in this disproportionate prosperity in a time of recession, namely the vast sums of LAUNDERED money in circulation from the multi-billion international trade in illicit drugs, which on a lower level accounts for much of the BLACK economy.

**Intelligentsia** No such word is to be found in the 1933 H–K volume of the OED although it had been used in English since before the Russian Revolution – part of every communist or anarchist revolutionary's verbal armoury of proletarian envy and class-hatred. It is the Russian adaptation (*intelligentsiya*) of the Latin word for 'intelligence', *intelligentia*. A later OED Supplement defines it with admirable evenhandedness as 'the part of a nation, originally in pre-revolutionary Russia, that aspires to intellectual activity; the class of society regarded as possessing culture and political initiative'. But Maurice Baring as early as 1907 wrote of the revolutionaries fearing '. . . a general massacre of the educated bourgeoisie' – something that was, at least in a modified form, to come true under Stalin. The British have never taken to the intelligentsia, except sardonically, preferring homelier words to insult each other with, such as 'intellectuals' or even 'highbrows'. However, 'longhaired' went out in the 1960s Beatles era.

**Inter-** A modish mid-20th-century prefix, probably brought into prominence by sociologists and other academics, who prefer 'interpersonal' to the simpler PERSONAL – though when two people have a close relationship it is unnecessary to describe it as 'personal' (e.g. 'a personal friend'), let alone 'interpersonal'. The advertising industry gave inter- a further boost, with the railways' renaming of long-distance trains as InterCity (at the same time providing another fashionable innovation, the IN-word capital letter, or else loss of letterspacing between words – and BBC Television introduced a silly SOAP known as *EastEnders*). Also the British Airways slogan word, 'BA Inter Britain', which proved to be an expensive mistake – when people inadvertently stressed the second syllable of 'inter', suggesting that the airline buried its customers. And the Open University does not offer 'breaks between courses' but 'intercourse breaks'.

**Intervention** A multi-purpose EURO-word. When farmers, vintners and other suppliers from countries belonging to the European Community find they have produced too much of whatever they grow or make, the Community intervenes by buying the surpluses and putting them in store so as to keep the price artificially high (hence the many 'wine lakes' and 'butter mountains'). Then, instead of giving the surplus produce to the poor or alleviating world-wide hunger, it is either kept 'in intervention' until it becomes unfit for consumption or is sold extremely cheaply to Russia, via CAPITALIST agents who, oxymoronically, are also Communists. 'Intervention' has, by extension, become a word meaning a store where such things are kept – in other words, it is a euphemism for one of the much-derided lakes or mountains mentioned above.

**Investigative journalism**  An aspect of CONSUMERISM pioneered by the American Ralph Nader, whose indefatigable research into unsafe American-made motor-cars revolutionised safety laws in that industry. And because federal laws introduced by his efforts demanded that motor-cars on American roads were safe whatever their country of origin, his work indirectly also affected road safety features built into motor vehicles by other countries whose manufacturers hoped to export their cars to the United States. Investigative journalism has also spread into commerce (e.g. food additives); and to politics, where it is more subjective. One of the hallmarks of investigative journalism is that the list of names appearing in the credits may sometimes be almost as long as the investigative article itself, and that the identity of WHISTLE-BLOWING informants is kept secret.

**It**  1) Sex, or sexual intercourse, as in 'I haven't had it for a month'. This is an old euphemistic meaning, dating from the 17th century or even earlier. 2) (Of a woman) sex appeal (see also OOMPH), in which sense it was used by Kipling in 1904, says the OED. 3) The end, especially in broadcasting, television or weather-forecasters' use as in 'That's *it* for tonight'. 4) Abbreviation of Italian Vermouth, as in 'Gin and It'. But most often, 5) More and yet more sex, sex appeal and sexual intercourse.

**I've started so I'll finish**  Catchphrase originating from the long-running BBC Television programme *Mastermind* (which is THE THINKING MAN'S television quiz – an oasis among idiot panel games). When a hooter signals a time-limit, the question-master always utters these words after being temporarily interrupted. Such is the power of television that the phrase has become part of English folk-speech and is applied to all kinds of situations, some of them obscene.

# J

**Jap** A common abbreviation of 'Japanese' to which some – not the Japs themselves – object on grounds of alleged racial disrespect, although it is a mere abbreviation of the proper word, not a derogatory one, like 'Nig' for 'Nigger' (see BLACK). The Japanese themselves in fact use the word as a neutral form of self-description in their own informal (English) writing, e.g. on tourist brochures, etc. – though not, as far as I know, 'Nips', which was a derogatory PROPAGANDA word during the Second World War (when there was much to be derogatory against the Nipponese for: I also recall seeing a suggestion that the word 'nylon' was an acronym for 'Now You Lousy Old Nips'.) The truth is that the Japanese, Nips or Japs don't care what people call them: they just get on with their work, relentlessly pursuing their national sport of raising the prosperity of their country – something the rest of us might do well to emulate. After all, the Jewish immigrants to Britain at the turn of the 20th century did much the same, without worrying OVERLY whether their hosts called them Yids, Moes, Kikes or even, euphemistically but inaccurately, described them as being 'of the oriental persuasion'. Asian immigrants, too, are too busy to worry about any slur-by-abbreviation, and Pakistanis accept the abbreviation Paki (except from the lips of the thugs who go 'Paki-bashing'). However, the practice of shortening racial or national group names can raise sensibilities which are delicate, if not always rational. Scottish people do not like to be called 'Scotch' or 'Scotchmen'; but 'Scots' or 'Scotsmen' is accepted (even by Scotswomen, in the more unspoilt and less anglicised parts of that beautiful country). During the last war 'Jerry' was an almost affectionate nickname for the German enemy (much less vicious than 'Hun' in the previous world war when there was, on the whole, less to be vicious about). Australians call their indigenous aboriginal countrymen 'Abos' in a matter-of-fact manner; but 'Chinks' or 'CHINEE' for Chinese people must be considered derogatory: even 'Chinaman' is frowned upon by those who feel it is patronising and best left to Victorian adventure stories. And the British themselves do not get very bothered about being called BRITS.

**(The) jewel in the crown (of . . .)**   I don't know who first described
India as the Jewel in the British Crown but after the phrase was
used as the title of a book by Paul Scott and later, in the mid-1980s,
by Granada Television for a fictional series based on it (and its
three companion-volumes), the title was pounced upon by all and
sundry and applied in the most ludicrous ways. Someone went
so far as to describe the British Rail toasted bacon sandwich as
'the jewel in the crown of our buffet car service'. (Soon afterwards
this popular item of fare was abolished and replaced by a
warmed-up bacon bun with the taste and texture of cotton-wool.)
There is a London wine bar, situated in a basement in Covent
Garden, named 'The Jewel in the Ground'.

**Jobs for the boys**   Personal or political nepotism, as exemplified
by the OLD BOYS' NETWORK. Nepotism, from Latin *nepos*, a nephew
(oddly also grandson), is defined as 'showing favour to one's
nephew or other close relative'. But there is more to it than that.
When Roman priests, bishops and popes fathered children they
were allowed, on due repentance, to describe them as nephews
and nieces, and, of course, saw to it that they obtained preferment.
As Robert Browning wrote, in *The Bishop orders his Tomb at
Saint Praxed's Church,* 'Nephews – sons mine . . . ah God, I know
not!'

**John Doe**   An anonymous, mythical average man who pursues
law-suits against the equally imaginary Richard Roe. See also
GEORGE SPELVIN and WALTER PLINGE.

**Joint**   A place, and, in combination with other words, a suffix
popularised in America in the early 1950s and soon adopted in
Britain, e.g. clip-joint, booze-joint, gay joint, etc., though it was a
cant word for a place or building in English slang from as early as
the 1820s. The cigarette containing cannabis is also called a joint,
and so in some circles is the hypodermic equipment used to
inject harder drugs. Nevertheless during the 1980s there was
formed in England a 'Joint Committee on the Misuse of Drugs'.

**Jolly hockeysticks**   Traditional description of a kind of hearty
English girl, a cheerful, outgoing, sports-loving, no-nonsense
sort of young woman, perhaps of the type exemplified by John
Betjeman's Joan Hunter Dunn (in *A Subaltern's Love-song*) who,

however, played a jolly game of tennis. Jolly hockeysticks girls come from upper or upper middle-class families, would in earlier times have COME OUT and traditionally vote Conservative.

**Journalism**   When the word SCIENTIST first entered British English in the middle of the last century there was a great outcry against it, as indeed there was even in the United States. But journalism, coming from the French word *journaliste* (officially declared valid by the *Académie Française* as early as 1718), was welcomed as a respectable immigrant: '"Journalism" is a good name for the thing meant ... A word was sadly wanted ...' wrote the *Westminster Review* in 1833. Nevertheless, journalists in France enjoyed (and some say still enjoy) a higher standing than they do in Britain, where their image has become tarnished by the emergence of the TABLOIDS (see also FLEET STREET). A journal was originally a *daily* record of events or of financial accounts, and thence became a favourite element in the naming of newspapers, not exclusively those published daily: 'weekly journal' soon ceased to be a paradox. A survey taken some years ago in America showed that 'Journal' was the third favourite title element (after 'News' and 'Times') among the thousands of newspapers published in the USA. The noun 'journalizer', meaning not a journalist in the above sense but one who enters a daily record in a journal or book, and the verb 'to journalize' sprang up in the 18th century but fell into disuse again in the 19th.

**Journo(s)**   Journalists call themselves and each other many names, including journos, scribes and, in a mock-self-deprecating way, hacks. Press photographers are photogs in the trade jargon.

**-Jungle**   Suffix denoting a sphere of (usually hectic and ruthless) activity which the speaker dislikes or disapproves of, e.g. the blackboard jungle (from the title of a book by Evan Hunter, made into a film in 1955), from which came various expressions such as the Fleet Street jungle, fast-food jungle, political jungle, race relations jungle, etc.

**Junior executive**   Office boy. See also EXECUTIVE.

**Junk-**   Vogue-prefix. Junk is a seafaring word of fine antiquity and uncertain derivation. It comes either from Latin *juncus*, a rush (though in its maritime associations more likely from the Spanish word, which is *junco*), or else from a word that preceded a chunk, or useless fragment. 'Hausers grete and small . . . Jonkes' – someone wrote in 1482. Because small left-overs of rope or hawser were too precious to waste they were made into fenders to protect ships from damage when they touched the quayside or each other, and these pads, too, were called junks. So the first junk shops were places where dirty old bits of rope and hemp were reworked, glued and woven together into once-more useful articles. An excellent precedent, therefore, for junk-food, with its re-formed gristle and ground-down bone masquerading as meat, and for junk-music, compiled from unpleasant chunks of repetitive rubbish and little merit, and doubtless for many other junk-prefix applications. (But see also PULP, for literary junk.) As a narcotic, the first recorded reference to junk is dated 1925, hence –

**Junkie** One who is addicted to illicit drugs (or, less often, one who peddles them, though these are often the same people, having to become dealers in order to finance their addiction). The OED says it is of 1920s coinage. See the analogous and more recent FOODIE; and also JOINT.

# K

**K** In the informal or jargon talk of businessmen, 'a thousand pounds', derived from computer language. Where men would formerly have said, 'I gave him ten GRAND' they may now vary it as 'ten kay'. This book (composed on an Apple Publishing System) contains about 500K.

**Kamikaze** From the Japanese *kami* = god + *kaze* = wind. In the year 1281 a strong gale destroyed a fleet of Mongolian ships that was about to invade Japan – much as the Spanish Armada was seen off by the English weather a few centuries later. The Japanese term 'wind of god' was adopted in the Second World War by Japanese bomber-pilots who purposely and suicidally crashed their planes on allied targets. After the war, with Japan safely defeated and humiliated, the word became the vehicle for many a joke, i.e. 'He's a failed kamikaze pilot . . .' etc., and a jocular prefix-word for foolhardy acts or enterprises, or anything risky – or indeed provocatively risqué, such as 'kamikaze knickers'.

**Kangaroo court** An informal or improvised trial without force of law, as for example one held by a group of workers in order to discipline one of their mates. At a different professional level, e.g. among doctors and lawyers, kangaroo courts are more grandly described as DISCIPLINARY TRIBUNALS. The earliest known kangaroo courts are recorded as having taken place in the middle of the 19th century in the United States, not, as one might expect, in Australia; and no-one seems to know why this harmless marsupial was singled out. Perhaps the primitive societies which hold kangaroo courts hark back to medieval times, when an animal, usually a dog, would be formally tried and hanged. There is, however, no analogy to the Horse Trial, in which the animal is tried in the sense of being tested against others. Kangaroo courts do, however, have much in common with SHOW TRIALS.

**Kosher nostra** The alleged Jewish MAFIA.

# L

**Lager** My own subjective English definition of the beverage would be a gaseous kind of beer containing artificially-added carbon dioxide bubbles, and bearing a much-advertised phoney, German-sounding name liberally sprinkled with meaningless *Umlaut* dots (see *The Joy of Words,* Elm Tree Books, 1986). Apart from inducing burps, lager may leave behind a sharp aftertaste of the tin-can it is sold in, disguised by the unnaturally cold temperature at which it needs to be drunk. English lager sometimes comes 'on draught' in pubs out of pumps (which add yet more gas when propelling it out of its metal barrel!) but more often in plastic-tied clusters of four or six cans with which the MACHO British male needs to festoon himself before he can contemplate a journey, football-match or other expedition. But 'lagering' is a word which has long been used by 20th-century English brewers and it comes from the German word *lagern,* to store or lay down. That in fact is what the Germans do to beer-in-cask, and they keep it in a *Lager* to age and clarify beer to the lightness they prefer. The slight cloudiness of our nice, tepid, English ale with fragments of hops and other matter floating in it, offends against their *Reinheitsgebot* (Purity Law). *Lager* is the ordinary German word for a store-house, encampment or camp. It was therefore also the normal abbreviated name for the German *Konzentrationslager*, the concentration-camps of the Nazi period; and is also present as the final element of the Russian acronym GULAG. Friedrich von Schiller (1759–1805) wrote a drama called *Wallensteins Lager*, whose name has so far not been appropriated by the English brewers.

**Laid back** American, early 1970s beatnik (see -NIK) term for anything or anybody who is considered to be pleasantly relaxed or easy-going – and, at first, by implication, one who has achieved that state by smoking a JOINT. Since then, however, even law-abiding, non-JUNKIE citizens can be described as laid-back.

**Lame ducks** Firms which are unable to 'stand on their own two feet', i.e. who are in financial difficulty. John Davies, Conservative Trade and Industry Secretary, speaking in the House of Commons on 4 November 1970, said, 'We believe that the essential need of the country is to gear its policies to the great majority of the people who are not lame ducks.' He was referring to a statement by Anthony Wedgwood Benn (a corresponding minister in a Labour Government), who had said on 1 February 1968, 'The next question is, what safeguards are there against the support of lame ducks.' In the succeeding years Labour and Conservative both supported and attacked the many millions of pounds they each poured into the bottomless purses of lame ducks, as it suited their respective political advantages. For another example of a SLOGAN that turned to bite its inventors see YESTERDAY'S MEN; also (THE) POUND IN YOUR POCKET.

**Laundering** The transferring of cash obtained through illicit dealings, e.g. in narcotics, or money obtained from robberies; either by temporarily placing it in foreign bank accounts or by entering into other gradual or piecemeal transactions so as to give such funds the appearance of having been legally obtained. See also STREET VALUE. But in some African countries, where many people carry their paper money about with them by putting it into their bras (if female) or under-pants (when worn, if male), laundering money has a different meaning. See also INSIDER DEALING.

**Lavatory** Euphemism, and an inaccurate one at that, for a TOILET.

**Leafletting** A new verb decribing the action of distributing advertising and other propaganda by leaflet, usually from house to house, as in the AIDS campaign. There is nothing wrong with creating new verbs from nouns. It happens all the time, but when the original noun ends in a single *t* the spurious addition of another one can make for uneasy formations reminiscent of bloodletting, etc. Perhaps the intention is to aid pronunciation and discourage people from reading 'leafleting' as 'lea-fleeting'.

**Left** The idea for dividing the political spectrum into left and right – and therefore necessarily also a CENTRE – was born in France at the end of the 18th century, when the more progressive, radical members of the National Assembly grouped themselves on the left-hand side of the president, and their opponents, the reactionaries, on the right. Those who felt less strongly committed to extremes naturally hedged their bets by sitting in the middle. Thus was born a large number of political descriptions, labels and *isms*. The left/right description did not really take hold in Britain until around the 1920s, and gained momentum with the Spanish Civil War as well as the rise of Nazism and Fascism. In America it still does not come naturally. This is partly because (as some leftists would allege) Americans naturally divide themselves into rightists and further-to-the-rightists. But they have a splendidly imaginative way of naming their political affiliations, for an account of which see William Safire's fine book, *The New Language of Politics* (Random House). In the British Houses of Parliament delegates and peers who are neither angrily to the left nor to the right but sit in the middle are oxymoronically called 'cross benchers' by the press – although they used to be properly called cross-benchers.

**Legendary** Legends are stories told and retold, handed down the ages and embellished. A legendary figure is usually considered to be an imaginary person. Today, however, legendary means simply very famous indeed, his attributes of fame also probably embellished. See also FABULOUS; and also the transformation of AWFUL from its original meaning.

**Leg man**  Among journalists, a reporter (not necessarily a man, although feminists are increasingly clamping down on such distinctions) who carries out the menial research for a features writer or reporter. The latter, however, gets most of the credit for the resulting work. It is becoming increasingly common for articles, especially in the SUNDAY PAPERS, to carry long lists of credits to as many as six reporters, generally INVESTIGATIVE, of whom some are bound to be leg persons, as they could hardly all crowd round the same typewriter. However, in vulgar men-talk (I'm a leg man – you're a tit man') the expression denotes alleged preferences of physical characteristics in sexual partners. See also FOOTMAN, and STRINGER, as well as other journalistic cross-references.

**Let it all hang out**  For a definition of this rather ambiguous exhortation to be relaxed, informal, probably noisy and offensive to bystanders, see DO ONE'S OWN THING.

**Liberation fronts**  Among civilised nations the recent trend has been to unite, e.g. the European Community (see EURO-). Elsewhere SEPARATISM is rife, with every ETHNIC group, every tribe (whether African or European) seeking self-determination. The underlying motives do not always stem from patriotism but may be rooted in a greed for power, with the inevitable corruption this brings. Most Liberation Fronts engage in TERRORISM.

**-like**  A downmarket suffix version of the IF-YOU-LIKE interjection.

**Listings**  All modern newspapers proudly let it be known that they carry these. But list*ings* are nothing more than *lists* prepared from information that is given to the papers free of charge by various interested bodies. These organisations get free publicity and the papers can fill their pages without having to pay journalists, and so everyone is happy – except perhaps the traditional newspaper-reader who prefers newspapers to print news.

**(The) .... Look**   Vogue suffix of commerce and fashion. Probably from the New Look in women's clothes which supplanted the years of austerity after the Second World War.

**Loony left**   In British politics, a derisive euphemism for a left-wing politics embracing a large variety of *isms* and *anti-isms* – from sexism and HETEROSEXISM to feminism, RACISM and consumerism to ageism and even ableism (all of which are treated either under their own heading or in the 'Forward'). The basic doctrine of loonies is seldom far removed from the many brands of outdated, juvenile or student communism rife in British politics and elsewhere – most of them impotent movements although some are so devoted to extreme leftism and the overturning of any kind of established order that they come full-circle and emerge as a particularly vicious kind of new fascism. Occasionally, as in the SOCIALIST Workers' Party and its splinter-groups (for no kind of politics suffers more from doctrinaire, internecine in-fighting than the loony left) some middle-aged or even elderly loonies may be encountered who are old enough to know better. In many parliamentary elections of the 1970s and 80s candidates from a self-styled Monster Raving Loony Party cheerfully lost their deposits in order to satirise the humourless political loonies. Although it may be considered actionable to describe someone as a lunatic (which is a synonym of 'insane') the description of 'loony' has so far not been tested in the courts. An interesting result of the rise of these loonies is that the term has been politicised, so that other words are used to describe ordinary, amiable, ineffectual silliness, e.g. WIMPS or WALLIES. See also MILITANT.

**Loopholes**   Originally holes in fortified walls to shoot through. But holes in walls are also useful for escaping, and thus the loophole soon became an outlet – or a let-out – in legal matters; or simply an excuse: 'Often applied to an ambiguity or omission in a statute, etc., which affords an opportunity for evading its intention.' (OED) – and, as Andrew Marvell wrote in about 1663, 'It would be below You and Me ... to have such loop-holes in our souls ... and to squeeze Our selves through our own words.'

**Love child** Media jargon for a child born out of wedlock, a bastard, perhaps to a COMMON-LAW WIFE, mistress, SPINSTER or SINGLE PARENT.

**Low key** Like SOFT PEDAL, a musical term absurdly misused by the MEDIA. There is no such thing as a 'low key' in music, though the term was occasionally printed on songs available in two or more transpositions, for low or high *voices,* and therefore marked either 'Low Key' or 'High Key'.

**Lubianka** (Also lubyanka) The notorious Moscow prison where political DISSIDENTS and other offenders are kept, but in transferred use, especially ironic or sarcastic, a reference to any building such as a place of work. Often used by journalists when mentioning the premises of rival papers. See PSYCHIATRIC HOSPITAL.

# M

**Macho** Pronounced 'match-oh': the ordinary Mexican-Spanish word for male or maleness, also applied to animals and plants. In the 1950s it was taken over by one or two American writers influenced by Mexican culture, and used at first in quotation-marks, but soon became a vogue-word among journalists. *Machismo* is also a legitimate Mexican-Spanish word and means the same thing, i.e. it is the related *ism* word.

**Macrobiotics** A health-food-faddists' vogue word. Everyone knows that 'micro' denotes small; most people know (thanks often to the admirable advocacy of health-food-faddists) that food that has been processed into a fine mess often has its goodness ground out of it, e.g. sugar, over-refined flour, etc.; and that eating rice, grain, etc., with the husks left on produces beneficial roughage. Hence the desirability of WHOLE food. This, it is thought, is the same as 'macro' (the opposite of 'micro' – hence 'big' food with the lumpy bits left in). It is not. The word 'macrobiotic' comes from the Greek words for long and life; and although the consumption of what is now described as macrobiotic food may well prolong life, macrobiotics is concerned with the prolongation of life in the wider sense, not just by healthy eating.

And this branch of science (or pseudo-science) has been around for a long time. Beethoven during the 1820s owned and read a copy of Hufeland's *Die Makrobiotik,* which was available in an English translation as long ago as 1797.

**Mafia** When the first edition of the OED was published in 1933, this Sicilian-Italian dialect word was explained as follows: 'In Sicily, the spirit of hostility to the law and its ministers prevailing among a large portion of the population, and manifesting itself frequently in vindictive crimes. Also, 'the body of those who share in this anti-legal spirit' which, the editors added, was 'often erroneously supposed to constitute an organised secret society existing for criminal purposes'. What made the editors so sure that this was erroneous is not clear, but in the 1976 supplement they were, of course, obliged to eat their words. The Sicilian and Italian *mafiosi* continued feuding and robbing, but large numbers of them emigrated to the United States, where they improved and consolidated their techniques. Theirs is very much a secret society, to which they refer conspiratorially and euphemistically as *cosa nostra* – 'our thing'. Hence, in facetious use, the Kosher Nostra, for an alleged Jewish conspiracy, or the Taffia for a Welsh one. And when, during the 1980s, the BBC appeared to have been taken over by a large number of brogue-wielding Irish broadcasters and TELEVISION PERSONALITIES, this invasion was by some attributed to the secret activities of an alleged Murphia.

**Mail(ing) shots** The sending-out of JUNK mail. See DIRECT MAIL.

**Man** When used as a form of address this includes woman, even among people (e.g. WIMMIN) who otherwise go out of their way to banish the 'man' and 'men' elements from everyday speech. It originates in American negro jazz musicians' slang and is still one of the characteristics of BLACK or pseudo-black speech. See also ALTERNATIVE, BREAD and their many cross-references.

**Marathon** Properly a race run over a distance of 26 miles 385 yards in imitation and commemoration of an ancient event that occurred near a *place* called Marathon, where the Persians were defeated by the Greeks. Now any event or activity which purports to test the participants' stamina or endurance is described as a marathon, even activities performed while seated and stationary.

What is more, the final element -(a)thon may be added to almost any word to suggest such an activity, or lack of, e.g. Sexathon, Eatathon, Talkathon, Musathon (!), etc. See also SPONSORSHIP.

**Marketing**  Most people would say that this is only another term for selling; but modern commerce and its academic theories have given it (and MERCHANDISING) a specialised meaning; in the same way as VENDING has become the action of selling something from a slot-machine.

**(The radio was playing) martial music**  The now traditional audible indication of something amiss in a BANANA REPUBLIC. Almost ever since broadcasting became recognised as a propaganda force the first objective of would-be revolutionaries has been to gain control of the radio station and claim to have taken over the government. And when they temporarily run out of lies a supply of records of 'martial music' seems always to be at hand. Although these now appear to be part of the stock-in-trade of every LIBERATION FRONT the invention can be credited to German teutonic thoroughness. Berlin radio played martial music in 1933 when Hitler's storm-troopers were marching, and so did the Austrian radio in 1934 during the abortive Nazi PUTSCH that resulted in the murder of Engelbert Dollfuss. But, curiously enough, when Hitler was holed up in his bunker in 1945 and the ghastly nightmare was about to meet its *Götterdämmerung* there was apparently no traditionally suitable music available. Not a note of Wagner issued forth from Berlin during that time: it was the music of the devoutly Christian Anton Bruckner which accompanied the evil housepainter's last hours. Today INDEPENDENT radio stations as well as BBC Radio 1 would no doubt continue pumping out their pop, oblivious of any events outside the CHARTS.

**Maudlin**  An aspersion on St Mary Magdalene, who is often depicted on old paintings as swollen-eyed and weeping tears of repentance (cynics say feigned ones) to express regret for having been a whore. Hence maudlin as a description of the mawkishly sentimental and, by extension, those tearfully drunk or 'in their cups' (see Horace: *Odes,* III, vi, 20). St Audrey is similarly calumnied in the word 'tawdry', because, at the annual fair held in honour of this saint in Ely, Cambridgeshire, cheap jewellery and a kind of neck-shawl of crude (or 'tawdry') lace would be sold or worn by women in the name of the saint.

**Maxi** See MINI-.

**Media** Now, in addition to the old-established meanings, a derogatory abbreviation of 'advertising media', 'news media', etc., but mostly meaning newspapers, radio and television. It is often pronounced and sometimes written 'meeja' – perhaps with conscious derision. The word is the plural of medium, but (like agenda, data and others, but not, as is sometimes alleged, PROPAGANDA) the singular use ('the media is . . .'.), based on the now almost universal neglect of Greek and Latin, is gaining ground. This is less objectionable when coming from the layman, whose usage will eventually prevail. But when bacteriologists, doctors or other scientific experts say, 'This bacteria is . . .'. or 'It is a common phenomena. . . .', or 'We must look for a different criteria . . .'. it is probably wise to be circumspect about their professional competence.

**Mega-** Greek for 'a million'. Popularised as a prefix by computer jargon (megabytes, etc.) and used to denote extremes, e.g. megaYUMMY, megasmelly, megalovely, etc. At present favoured by YUPPIES but by the time this paragraph appears in print their tastes and catchwords will doubtless have changed.

**Merchandising** A form of selling. See also MARKETING.

**Message** Like 'break', this is a disc-jockeys' and general INDEPENDENT (i.e. COMMERCIAL) television and radio euphemism for a paid-for advertisement, as in 'We'll be back after the break . . .' or 'See [!] you . . . after this message . . .'. See also ANNOUNCEMENT and DEDICATION.

**Mexican wave** A crowd phenomenon seen on television screens all over the world during the 1986 World Cup in Mexico. Spectators would rise from their seats in turn and sit down again, but in a corporately, informally organised progressive manner, which gives the impression from a distance of an undulating wave making its way round the stadium. On the terraces of British football grounds, where spectators do not sit but stand, the wave is lateral, as the crowd surges forward in an alarming way.

**Militant** Abbreviated from Militant Tendency (also for a time tendentiously known as 'The Tendency'): since the early 1980s, a subversive left-wing political party within a left-wing political party, usually but not always the Labour Party. 'Militant' refers to the extremist socialist/communist/militant views of its adherents; but the second word (often now omitted) is the more significant, very well chosen by people who do not normally care much for the meaning of words. In old English, a 'tender' was simply a person who attended. This is how the Militant Tendency achieved its objects and gained control of the branches it infiltrated. Many constituency parties are small, with a number of members who, because of their moderate views, often fail to attend meetings. Thus it has always been a simple matter for extremists to drum up support among friends and relations and thus gain control – simply by bothering to attend, while their more apathetic colleagues were watching television at home. This process is also known as democracy. A newer word is entryism.

**Mini-** Vogue prefix fashionable from 1960 for anything small or miniature, a fashion started by the Mini car made by the Morris and Austin motor companies (1959) and by the advent of the miniskirt. (Skirt manufacturers as well as the car companies subsequently also produced a Maxi.) But neither the car-makers nor the dress-designers invented the prefix, which was first used (and patented) by the English piano maker W. G. Eavestaff, who in 1932 introduced a new kind of dwarf piano, 2 ft. 9 inches high, which he registered as the Minipiano. From 1946 the English composer Geoffrey Hartley composed a series of small cantatas for amateur performance called (with reference to the Eavestaff product) Minicantatas. The success of the prefix may be not unconnected with the fact that *min-* in Celtic had associations with small size, and there are various other related ancient forms, including *minion,* which (although now meaning a menial servant) was originally a term of endearment, like 'darling', or 'beloved'. For an earlier miniaturising term see TABLOID.

**Mister** Prefix of American origin, usually with faintly sardonic or even sarcastic overtones, e.g. Mister Big, Mister Clean, Mister

Wonderful. Also used by publicity agents as names for their clients – Mister Piano, Mister Magic, etc., with the implication that they personify the ultimate, the STATE OF THE ART, in their particular field.

**M'lud**  The correct form of address for judges above a certain rank (when not addressed as 'Your Honour'): 'M'lud', not 'my lord'. Exchange in court. *Barrister:* 'The defendant was drunk as a judge.' *Judge:* 'I thought the expression was "drunk as a Lord".' *Barrister:* 'Sorry, M'lud!' See also HOORAY HENRYS.

**-mobile**  A vehicle, the prefix determining its kind, e.g. snowmobile, Popemobile, dullsmobile, beachmobile, etc. An American slang extension of the original automobile.

**Monetarism**  The doctrine of exercising a tight control on the money supply for the prevention of, or as a remedy against, inflation. See also THATCHERISM, which is largely based on monetarism, and BUTSKELLISM, which was a rare phenomenon in British politics.

**Monkeys and organ-grinders**  A common political analogy, used in much the same way as the POLITICAL POODLE comparison coined by David Lloyd George in 1907. During the LOONY political disaster that overtook Liverpool politics during the 1980s, when the aged, experienced (and by inclination moderate) leader of the Labour council stood silently by while his young deputy endlessly repeated SLOGANS and platitudes, the older man was always described as playing the monkey to the younger man's organ-grinder. This kind of picture is very familiar now from numerous television news and current-affairs programmes, when ordinary citizens, usually husband-and-wife, are interviewed about something they witnessed or experienced: one does all the talking, while the other awkwardly stares into space or nods approval.

**Montezuma's revenge**  See AZTEC TWO-STEP.

**Mooning**  Baring the buttocks as a form of insult or protest, said to be an old custom among Maori males. The word was popularised after the Queen was repeatedly exposed to this

spectacle during a visit to New Zealand in 1986. Maori females
(or their supporters) took to exposing their breasts instead. But
the *Guardian* (22 March 1974) claimed that mooning was
American and was the female equivalent of streaking, a 'practice
that cropped up in campuses across the United States in the late
fifties and early sixties.... Mooning consisted ... of exposing the
bottom in the general direction of whoever the mooner wanted
to impress, protest to or affront.' It is not connected with the
'Moonies', a wicked pseudo-religious cult founded by an Asian
man surnamed Moon.

**Moonlighting**  Illicit activities carried on under cover of darkness
but with help from the light of the moon have a long history. 'In
Ireland (says the OED), the perpetration by night of outrages...'
Later (from the beginning of the 20th century) it referred to the
Moonlight Flit, or leaving a place of residence without paying the
rent; but more recently (from the 1950s) the taking of two jobs.
There is nothing illicit about this, except that the tax collector
usually knows nothing about the second job – nor indeed often
about the first.

**MOR**  Abbreviation of Middle of the Road, generally when
applied to pop music of the MUZAK sort.

**Moral victory**  Loser's euphemism for a defeat. As when the
Islington Council Leader said, 'It was a moral victory for us despite
the judge's decision against us.'

**Motivation**  One of many newly-desirable but nebulous qualities
often demanded in job advertisements. A person who is
'motivated' will work to achieve his desired goal – though it could
well be that of getting his hand in the firm's till as quickly as
possible. He will also be 'committed' – to whom or what is never
specified – and strive to be a HIGH-FLYER. Salesmen may be
required to possess the kind of qualities that enable them to be
described as 'aggressive'; though that means not rude to
customers but to be 'motivated and totally committed'. 'Self-
starters' are also frequently advertised for. These have nothing
to do with motor-cars but have the ability to work on their own
without being 'motivated' by superiors.

**Motoring** This must now be classed as an archaism. 'To motor' was a coinage used by many (and disapproved of by many more) when the motor-car was in its ascendancy ('I'll motor you to the station . . .'). There was even a brand of chocolate sold under this name, so new and strange and desirable was the car. That was at a time when 'driving' still meant horse-drawn transport, and a distinction had to be made. But now that this has all but disappeared, driving means in a motor-car (except to the sporting carriage specialist), and doing so as quickly as possible to get from one place to another. Motoring up to the late 1950s still carried suggestions of the motor-car used for leisure and holidays, and as a means of visiting interesting places. The word carriage suffered a like transformation from the horse-drawn to the railways and motor-car.

**Ms** The unpronounceable courtesy prefix which, when added to a surname, is meant to conceal whether the woman so described is married, divorced or a SPINSTER; and which, when she uses the title herself, has strong feminist or none-of-your-business implications. The nearest one can get to pronouncing 'Ms (a kind of noncommittal compromise between 'Miss' and 'Mrs') is to buzz like a wasp. The OED Supplement says it is 'increasingly common but not universally accepted', which is a NICE understatement. Ms first appeared in America during the early 1950s, with the rise of what was then still called Women's Lib(eration) but is now feminism. It may have been a subconscious modification of the old American 'Miz', a rustic dialect pronunciation of Mrs – which is, of course, itself a corruption of the ancient English 'Mistress', a courtesy title applicable in the 17th and 18th centuries to both married and unmarried women. See also COMMON LAW WIFE.

**Mugging** In American negro slang a mug used to be the same as a chap, i.e. a man or a person: 'De mug what plays de flute has de music all t'himself when de odder mugs in de orchestra don't do nottin'.' (E. W. Townsend, 1895.) But there are numerous other instances quoted in the OED with the connotation of fighting between two people, and – chiefly in American English – to rob with violence. Before violent mugging was brought to the streets of urban Britain, it meant, in Liverpool Scouse, treating someone to a free drink or meal, e.g. 'I'll mug yer' (see *Lern Yerself Scouse*, Scouse Press, 1964 onwards).

**Murphia** See MAFIA.

**Music centre** A new-fangled substitute for the formerly new-fangled RADIOGRAM. See CENTRE.

**Muzak** The origin of the name for continuous 'piped' music actually lies in the success of the box BROWNIE camera. Room's *Dictionary of Trade Name Origins* (Routledge) says the name was first registered by Rediffusion in the *Trade Marks Journal* in 1938 – 'combining *Kodak* and "music" '. Muzak is background music which its promoters claim to be unobtrusive and at the same time reassuring to the hearer, but the best that can be said for it is that it is MOR and therefore not as great an abomination as the continuous rock music which infests shops, pubs, restaurants and other public places. There are signs that the *-zak* ending is becoming belatedly fashionable for things considered to be WALL-TO-WALL, judging from increasing appearances in the press, e.g. 'talkzak', 'news-zak' and 'chat-zak' used by different writers on adjacent pages of the *Listener* (2 April 1987): thus written, and evidently sub-edited, by different hands!

**'My guest(s) today ...'** The almost invariable but inaccurate opening gambit of every television or radio host of chat-shows (which the Americans, incidentally, less derisorily call 'talk-shows'). When the host says '*my* guest' he refers to people about whom usually he knows no more than what he sees in the script before him, which has been compiled for him by RESEARCHERS. Most listeners and viewers are only too well aware that these programmes depend on a great deal of teamwork and many a GHOST, so why not be honest and say, '*Our* guest'?

# N

**'N'** The overdone commercial abbreviation of 'and', as in mix'n' match; from the American, and based on sign-writers' needs for cramming big messages into small spaces. Often seen on menus, where even the oldest-established English dishes have succumbed to this Americanism, e.g. fish'n'chips, egg'n'tomato, sausage'n'beans, etc.

**Name** Apart from the common meaning, since about 1880 a kind of self-effacing euphemism for someone so rich that he can gamble large sums on the London insurance market. The minimum sum a Name must be able to invest, and risk losing (although the gains are usually disproportionately immense) is at present £100,000. Many famous TELEVISION PERSONALITIES, whose fame is sometimes ephemeral and therefore itself a giant gamble, become Names at Lloyds.

**Nanny state** Derisive description of the WELFARE STATE, usually from men of the ultra-Conservative RIGHT (or dries) in whose formative years the nanny probably played an unduly formative role in their later lives – a role that could range from gentle cosseting to corporal punishment. Also, 'to nanny – to act in the manner of a nanny, to be unreasonably protective' (OED).

**Natural resurface control programme** United States Army and PENTAGONESE euphemism for the chemical defoliation of trees. See also AIR SUPPORT and other cross-references.

**.... needs you** The magazine *London Opinion* on 5 September 1914 had a cover showing Field Marshall Lord Kitchener fixing the beholder with steadfastly staring eyes and pointing an accusing finger, with the caption, 'Your Country needs YOU'. This was later reproduced by the Parliamentary Recruiting Committee, became the most famous war PROPAGANDA poster of all time and has been endlessly parodied. It should be added that there was then no general conscription, and all Britons who served in the forces during the earlier part of the First World War were volunteers.

**Negative** Bad, as in 'negative publicity'.

**Neighbourhood** Civic and municipal neologist prefix word used, like COMMUNITY, more for its sound than its inherent meaning, as in Neighbourhood/Community Action, Neighbourhood/Community Amenities, Neighbourhood/Community CENTRE, etc. Unfortunately such descriptions seldom indicate any increased neighbourly feelings or neighbourhood AWARENESS. But see also FRIENDLY NEIGHBOURHOOD.

**Network** A word in fashionable use, its undue popularity probably derived from television, where programmes that are seen on all channels (of one sort or the other – COMMERCIAL or BBC) are 'on network', or 'networked'. It has become a favourite title element in entertainments, usually those offered by travelling or touring performers, e.g. the Classical Music Network, the Contemporary Poetry Network, Ballet Network, etc. Network also features in some of the periodic name-changes indulged in by British Rail (formerly British Railways). For example, what began factually as Southern Railways and became British Rail(ways) Southern Region is now Network South East, though the snappy title has not improved services or resulted in cleaner trains. But see also OLD BOY NETWORK and WORKSHOP.

**Nice** This all-purpose word is a living, one-syllable example of the way the language has changed. In the 14th and 15th centuries, the OED tells us, it meant foolish, stupid or senseless, as well as wanton, loose-mannered or lascivious. Then its meaning changed to trim, elegant and smart, as applied to extravagant or ostentatious dress: as Caxton wrote in the *Golden Legend* (1483), 'She chastysed them that were nyce and queynte, sayeing that suche nycete was fylthe of the sowle.' Other definitions include strange, rare, uncommon, towards the 16th century, slothful, lazy, indolent; and then, effeminate, unmanly, tender, delicate (as might now be burlesqued with the lisping pronunciation 'nithe'). In the 17th century nice meant over-refined, luxurious – perhaps affectedly so (as in today's sarcastic 'quaite naice'), followed by definitions meaning accuracy, strictness and precision (hence the surviving nicety, or 'a nice distinction', which means a fine distinction, not a pleasing one). Only in the 18th century did nice begin to mean agreeable, pleasant or attractive in the way it is used today. Now everything can be described as nice that is clever or pleasing and not nasty – even a goal or other effective manoeuvre in football: 'Nice one, Cyril!'

**-nik** The Russian suffix-of-association, transferred via Jewish and Yiddish usage into American, and thence into English, often with facetious intent. In Russian it may be compared to the English -er ending, e.g. one who farms is a farmer (see also -STER). The Russians in 1957 launched their first space satellite and (having no indigenous word for satellite) named it *sputnik*, which means

FELLOW-TRAVELLER (a word which, quite fortuitously, already had a communist-sympathising meaning in English). But long before that, Yiddish-speakers in America as well as the rest of the world had their *nudnik* (a pest, a bore, a tedious fellow). Beatniks were those of the 'beat generation' who modelled themselves on Gertrude Stein's 'lost generation' but were rather smellier and more unwashed than would have appealed to her sensibilities. (At first they were also called 'beatsters' – see above.) America soon went crazy about the -nik suffix, calling Bach-lovers Bachniks, cobblers shoeniks, those associated with psychoanalysis Freudniks, etc.; and countless other combinations – gayniks and straightniks, folkniks and peaceniks. The formation seems to work best with short words: a meatnik is the opposite of a vegetarian, but the latter has no -nik to his name. An alrightnik is a person prosperous enough to be able to say he has 'done all right', etc., etc.

**Nuclear family**  A prime example of the word-blindness that often afflicts the social scientist. A sociologist might rail against nuclear weapons and then, in the same breath, extol the nuclear family, by which is meant a father, a mother, and their child or children. See also EXTENDED FAMILY.

**Nudge-nudge wink-wink**  A conversational aid to indicate sexual suggestiveness, or a kind of verbal dig-in-the-ribs, e.g., 'They went on holiday together, you know, nudge-nudge wink-wink.' See also HOW'S YOUR FATHER.

**O'-**  The facetious 'Irishising' prefix, e.g. an Irish author's adaptation of Flaubert's *Madame Bovary* nicknamed 'Emma O'Bovary'. The mock-Scottish 'Mac-' is also occasionally used, but not as commonly as the Russianising suffix -SKI.

**-o**  This suffix is said by some to have its origin in the Scouse dialect of Liverpool, where it has certainly been fashionable as a diminutive longer than elsewhere in Britain. People who would be named or nicknamed 'Tommy' or 'Jackie' or 'Kid' in the rest of Britain have in living memory been often called Tommo, Jacko or Kiddo in Liverpool, although ammunition has been 'ammo' in the British army since its soldiers were known as Tommies (never Tommoes!). But the -o movement has also long enjoyed popularity in America, perhaps springing from mock-Spanishisms, with dumbo, queero, socko, lesbo, limo and many others. In Britain, PINKOS and weirdos (not to be confused with hairdos) often figure in the more informal pages of the press, especially among diarists and gossip columnists, though these usually disagree about the spelling of the plural: wino's, winos or winoes? See also DEMO.

**Obscene** From the Latin *obscenus*. This was in earlier English usage the word for things or events inauspicious, adverse, unfavourable or ill-omened. In Shakespeare's time it meant anything disgusting, loathsome, foul or objectionable, though not necessarily sexually so. In the succeeding centuries the unchaste, sexual connotations crowded out the original meanings. But in modern use, perhaps since the 1960s, almost anything a speaker (at any rate some speakers) might disapprove of can be hyperbolically described as obscene – especially wages offers (when these are not 'derisive'). See also EXPLICIT.

**-ocracy** Suffix formed from the Greek *kratein,* to rule, but adapted from the best-known 'rule' word, democracy (i.e. rule by the people). Many more or less absurd formations have appeared, like meritocracy, jazzocracy, Toryocracy, popocracy, etc.; but not, so far, pollexocracy (rule of thumb). For a similar fad see -HOLIC.

**.... of shame** Cliché coined by FLEET STREET as a way of making mundane stories appear more dramatic, e.g. by describing a house in which two scoutmasters mildly misbehaved as a 'House of Shame'. The expression has mercifully now been almost killed off by satire, after *Private Eye* neatly turned it against the press by calling FLEET STREET itself 'the Street of Shame' – which in many ways it was and in some ways still is.

**.... of the Year** A clever if blatant way of advertising, and for the MEDIA to draw attention to each other and themselves by mutual back-patting.

**-ogram** See -GRAM.

**Oh yeah?** See TELL THAT TO THE MARINES.

**OK** Correct, good, yes, I agree with you, all right (or 'alright'),
in good health ('How are you?' 'OK, thanks'), my glass is still full,
or, I don't want any more to drink ('Have another drink?' 'I'm OK,
thanks') and many other applications to denote positive qualities
or agreement. There is also the LAID BACK modification, 'Oke':
Richard Church, in *The Spectator* (1935), wrote, 'A child replied
"oke" to something I said. After a shudder of dismay, I reflected
that this telescoped version of "O.K.", now used to mean "Right
you are", or "I agree", or any other form of assent, will ultimately
appear in the textbooks as a legitimate word, with an example
quoted from a poet who is at present mute and inglorious.' As for
its origins, all that is certain is that it is an Americanism and dates
from about 1840. OK has been explained in a great variety of ways
by many authorities, e.g. the OED and H. L. Mencken, with more
or less far-fetched suggestions: as the abbreviation of a facetious
spelling of 'all correct', 'orl korrekt' or 'oll korrekt'; as the
abbreviated nickname 'Old Kinderhook', the name of an
American Democratic candidate in the presidential election of
1840; as a member (and therefore considered a socially
acceptable person) of the prestige-laden O.K. Club of New York
City, founded before 1840; from the French *aux quais* 'used in the
American War of Independence by Frenchmen who made
appointments with American girls'; from a Choctaw Indian word,
*oke,* or *hoke,* for 'yes, it is'; from the Finnish word *oikea,* meaning
correct; from an American firm by name of Orrins-Kendall which
always put its initials on packing-cases to let its customers know
that the contents had been carefully inspected and passed as –
well – OK; from the theory that old, post-Norse, Scandinavian
sailors proclaimed themselves and their vessels *hofgor,* i.e.
'ready for the sea', abbreviated 'hg', which is in those languages
pronounced 'hoh gay'; from a Prussian general and supreme
commander who initialled documents with the first letters of
*Oberst Kommandant*; from the Scottish *och aye* corrupted to 'ok-
aye' by lowlanders unable to pronounce the guttural Scots *ch*;
from *o-ke* ('it is so') in the Djabo dialect of Liberia; from *hoak-keh*
in Burmese, meaning the same thing; an abbreviation of the
Greek ola-kala; and (an English explanation) that certain

documents in the House of Lords required the initials of Lords
Onslow and Kilbracken, who jointly annotated them 'O.K'. In
Britain the use of OK was further spread not only by American
films but also by the food manufacturers Mason (now part of a
larger conglomerate) who many years ago introduced bottled
flavour-enhancing (some say flavour-disguising) table condiment
with the trade-name OK Sauce. So take your pick. A sinister
modern use of OK can be seen in graffiti and other popular
utterances by the otherwise illiterate and inarticulate, such as
'Niggers out OK'; or 'Chelsea rule OK'; or 'George Davis is
innocent OK'. This kind of OK has to be spoken with a truculently
questioning, rising inflexion, as if to say, 'Disagree with me at
your peril.'

**-ola** American slang suffix of Italian origin, 'usually a decorative
lengthening giving slangy, colloquial or flippant connotations',
according to Wentworth & Flexner, who cite 'whamola – a very
successful gag' and 'flopola', presumably the opposite. Best
known in the United Kingdom through PAYOLA. See also the -O
suffix.

**Old boy network** Age is relative, and nowhere more so than in
extreme youth. A schoolboy in his teens considers old a former
fellow-pupil only a few years older but who has left school to enter
the world or higher education. In the English PUBLIC SCHOOL system
these young grown-ups are always known as old boys, whether
aged eighteen or eighty; and the same adjective is applied to
girls, of course. Some say that there is a kind of freemasonry of
mutual loyalty among former school-mates, who may be close
friends or, as strangers, identify each other's educational
provenance by recognising their 'old school tie' – and then
perhaps show favours, or give preference in employment. See
also NETWORK.

**On account (of)** Americanism for 'because'. One of many
examples of the German-inspired longwindedness that has taken
hold in American English. As S. P. Duschinsky wrote in the
magazine *New Society* (4 July 1974): 'Nixon is deprived on
account of he is not depraved.' See also PENTAGONISMS.

**On a daily basis** Americanism for 'daily': the same remarks
apply as above.

**On a global basis/scale** Ditto – 'worldwide'.

**One-liner** A kind of quip, joke or repartee often found in SITCOM, or written for and delivered by radio presenters who read them as if they were their own. Perhaps related to the old 'Penny-a-liner', which was the derisory name for a FLEET STREET hack who used flowery and circumlocutory prose (some of which has become, and still is, part of news language). It arose because 19th-century journalists were often paid by the line, a practice which encouraged prolixity. The following comment appeared in the *Musical Times* of 1 May 1893: 'Curious English appears in some New York papers. When a scribe of the *Sun* wished to say that "whistling fiends" are a frequent nuisance, he put it that they "infest the environment of daily life". Paid by the line, we imagine.'

**One man and his ....** Headline and title cliché, from a television series entitled *One Man and his Dog,* concerning English sheepdogs – after which there was for a time no stopping the numerous men who did this or that with companions or objects of their choice.

**Ongoing** Businessmen's favourite jargon word meaning continuing, continuous, in progress etc. but recorded in the OED as having been current – though not fashionable – since 1877. See also SITUATION.

**On stream** To 'come on stream' means generally to start working, to come into force or operation, whether liquids are involved or not. From the jargon of the oil industry, said of the long-awaited moment when the oil starts flowing.

**Oomph** A woman who has this has sex appeal (though not necessarily beauty, which oomph can replace or amplify) and is extremely attractive – not only sexually to men but also appreciated by women, for possessing a vitality, glamour and dress-sense, etc. In another word, she has IT.

**Operative** (Noun) GENTEELISM/euphemism for a worker. Today's Karl Marx would invite the operatives of the world to unite.

**Orchestrate**  In music, orchestration is the action of disposing various instruments into a score – though generally only a score for more than a dozen or so instruments: a sonata or string quartet is scored, not orchestrated. In MEDIA jargon to orchestrate something means to organise it, or cause something to happen, sometimes by cunning and/or stealth, e.g. 'carefully orchestrated in a LOW KEY'.

**Oreo**  A Negro who adopts the life-style and values of the white ESTABLISHMENT which, it is implied, he secretly wishes to join. It comes from the trade-name of an American chocolate 'cookie' with a vanilla filling – that is to say, it is black outside but white within. See also UNCLE TOMISM, AFRO-SAXON.

**Organic**  The word has recognised chemical, physical and biological meanings but these are of no concern to the believer in WHOLE food, who uses the word as a shorthand way of describing foodstuffs which have been allegedly 'grown without the help of chemical fertilisers'. And as such, 'organic' has become a modern BUZZWORD. While this movement towards healthier eating has achieved many victories over greedy farmers and growers for whom the size and quantity of produce is more important than wholesomeness, in practice 'organic' vegetables may often be recognised only by the large amount of mud and earth that is sold with them.

**Organiser**  (Sometimes Personal Organiser) A new word for an old idea – a big and bulky loose-leaf diary favoured by YUPPIES and containing a large number of different inserts, compartments and pockets. They are so big that they cannot be carried in the pocket but must be dragged around in EXECUTIVE briefcases.

**-orium**  Shops' suffix, of American origin, where the archaic Emporium led to more or less facetious coinages like Barbertorium, Drinkatorium, Libr(it)orium, etc. See also CENTRE and FORNICATORIUM, which will lead you to the DIRTY MAC BRIGADE.

**Orthopaedic**  From two Greek words meaning 'straight child': *ortho-* being the prefix denoting correctness. From this the medical profession has derived a large number of useful terms applicable to persons of all ages. But when the manufacturers of

mattresses and beds describe their products as 'orthopaedic' all
they mean is that these are hard and support the reclining human
body without allowing it to sag into depressions. See also THERMAL
underwear.

**Out out out!**   War-cry of RENTACROWD demonstrators, usually
uttered during DEMOS in jingling repetition and preceded by a
reiteration of whatever or whoever it is they wish to oust, e.g.
'Maggiemaggiemaggie, Out out out!'

**Out there**   A place where things are thought to happen in which
the speaker has a strong interest but plays little or no part. Thus
a football manager might say to his team before a match, 'Get out
there lads and play,' and afterwards, 'The opposition out there
was too strong for us'; or a policeman, interviewed on the radio,
said, 'My men out there have an arduous and difficult task.'
Probably derived from the jargon of war, where those who direct
operations are usually under cover and in comparative safety.

**Overkill**   A favourite PENTAGONISM meaning to kill more people or
destroy more things than is necessary in order to achieve the
desired military objective. Nuclear weapons are the best
examples of overkill, but the word was much employed in the
Vietnam War. Also used figuratively or facetiously to mean any
kind of exaggerated rules, measures or recommendations, e.g.
anti-racists' banning of all uses of the word BLACK, as in trades
union blackings and blacklegging, and even the nursery-rhyme
*Baa, Baa Black Sheep,* which is by some LOONY overkillers now
recommended to be sung as '. . . *Green Sheep*'. (See Colour
Supplement.)

**Overly**   Americans, with the taste for using longer words where
shorter ones would do, prefer this to over-, unduly, as in 'overly
anxious' for over-anxious.

**Over-policing**   A word that has been politicised and which has
in recent years changed sides, from being a good, POSITIVE one,
to something approaching to a term of abuse and complaint. The
indisputable fact is that all law-abiding British citizens (who in
any case seldom use the word) would *like* to be 'overpoliced',

with a policeman stationed at every street-corner and, if possible, several patrolling their gardens at night.

**Over the moon** People who so describe themselves are very happy, possibly even ON CLOUD NINE or in the SEVENTH HEAVEN. But see also SICK AS A PARROT.

**Own goal** From football slang, but used in politics as well as TERRORISM: a self-inflicted injury, as when (to the relief of all civilised people) a terrorist blows himself up with his own device instead of hurting the innocent. 'Shooting oneself in the foot' is an older expression, derived from the English sport of killing wild animals, and similarly used in a figurative sense.

# P

**Packaging** A phenomenon of the leisure and entertainment industry by which almost anything or anybody – authors, singers, pianists, etc. – can be made saleable and even desirable, and indeed turned into authors, singers, pianists, etc. Many books bearing famous names are written for them. After the success of the Beatles (an early example of minimal musical talent packaged by managers and musical GHOSTS) an American pop group called the Monkees (the name chosen with allusion to the fact that even monkeys can be packaged) achieved an enormous but purposely artificial success; and so did a female pop group assembled for a television series from three actresses who convincingly imitated pop 'stars'. And a personable young pianist of modest ability was taken up by an entrepreneur, renamed 'Richard Clayderman' and packaged into commercial fame and success by the expedient of getting his records plugged in television advertisements.

**Paedophile** Euphemism invented by an association of criminal pederasts in order to lend themselves an air of respectability. According to the two Greek elements from which paedophile is formed the word means 'lovers of children'. Pederast comes from much the same roots but in this sense the p(a)ed- prefix denotes boys rather than children, and is usually defined as the

criminal buggery of male minors; which is why 'paedophiles' felt
they needed to make a new word.

**Page three** The page on which TABLOID newspapers often print
pictures of near-naked women, known as 'Page Three Girls'.
However, a newspaper as old-established and conservative as
the *Daily Telegraph,* while spurning photographs of bare
breasts, usually manages to find at least one salacious story
(usually several) for its third page.

**Paper tiger** The symbolic term for a person or country that puts
on an outward show of strength or aggression but has no power
to back any threat with action. First used by CHAIRMAN Mao in 1946,
when he said to an American newspaperwoman, 'All
reactionaries are paper tigers. In appearance, the reactionaries
are terrifying, but in reality they are not powerful.' See also
REACTIONARY.

**Park** Old meaning: an open space, usually in public ownership,
used for recreation and amusement. New meanings include, in
football slang, the field of play; a place where cars are parked;
and most recently, a pretentious name for an industrial estate:
Kirkby Industrial Park, Wavertree Technology Park, etc. And a
news-item in *The Times* reports that 'Harefield Hospital in West
London is to set up what is claimed to be the world's first medi-
park.' See also THEME PARK.

**Payola** From pay + the American-Italian-OLA suffix (which please
see). This is one of the many unattractive faces of modern pop
music. Payola is a euphemism for the bribery that may occur in
one form or another between disc-jockeys and pop-record
producers. One of the chief characteristics of pop records is the
ephemeral nature of their appeal – sometimes no more than four
or five weeks in the CHARTS; and the riches that can be gained from
a record by high-pressure sales during its short life are quite
disproportionate to its musical merit. Much pressure is therefore
put on those who have the power to promote a new record by
playing it; and, not surprisingly, inducements may be offered.
These are not necessarily financial but may involve gifts in kind,
or even the services of prostitutes – as was shown during the
notorious Payola Trial during the 1970s, when Britons learnt a lot

about the seamier side of the music industry – not to mention the meaning of PLATING.

**Pee** Apart from the common euphemistic abbreviation for passing urine, an abbreviation for the 'new' British penny: as in 'I paid six pee', when previously people would always have said 'sixpence'. They never said 'six pee', nor indeed 'six dee'. See also (THE) POUND IN YOUR POCKET.

**Pentagonisms/pentagonese** The Americans have an admirable capacity for inventing original and stimulating additions to the English language, and some of them may be found scattered in these pages. But they also perpetrate almost literal translations of longwinded German absurdities – as the influence of that language on American English is second only to British English. Thus, an American who is asked a formal question will always try to avoid the simple 'yes' (or 'no') and instead reply, 'The answer is in the affirmative (or negative).' Pentagonese also enshrines many euphemisms, e.g. 'Tactical Air Support' for bombing, DESTABILISATION (of both potential enemies' as well as legitimate administrations) for subversion, 'Intelligence' for spying, etc. General Alexander Haig (1924–), in his capacity of Chief of Staff at the White House from 1973 to 1974, and in other official appointments, showed a wondrous flair for coining circumlocutory pentagonisms and was rewarded with the coining of a special word, 'Haigspeak'. Without the least selfconsciousness he could utter phrases like 'exacerbating mutual restraint' and speak of 'an additional number of augmentees'; and invent verbs like 'to context and to caveat'. In 1981 he won the American Doublespeak Award.

**People's** Prefix word (as in People's Republic, People's Court, People's Tribunal, etc.) indicating a totalitarian regime or one of its malpractices in which power is effectively removed from the ordinary people. The early English SOCIALISTS toyed with the word when it was still respectable, and for many years Whitechapel in the East End of London has proudly supported a concert and meeting hall with the apparently oxymoronic name, The People's Palace.

**Perk** Abbreviation of perquisite, which comes from Latin *per + quisitum,* 'that which is diligently searched for or asked after', and can be anything from a monetary tip to a special benefit awarded without being earned by the receiver. There are also old legal meanings, i.e. 'casual profits that come to the lord of a manor in addition to his regular annual revenue', and even 'property acquired otherwise than by inheritance' (a nice legal euphemism for theft?). But the following definition of perks was offered as early as 1869: 'The species of dishonesty alluded to is called by the cant name of "perks" ... and shows itself a word of amazing flexibility. It applies to such unconsidered trifles as wax candle ends, and may be stretched so far as to cover the larcenous abstraction by our man-servant of forgotten coats and vests.' Today's perks range from expensive FREEBIES enjoyed by journalists to PAYOLA company cars, GIRL FRIDAYS and 'personal assistants', down to free paper-clips, ballpoint pens and private telephone calls made 'on the house'. These are commonly taken from (and often freely given by) employers. Perks are not related to 'perky', which now describes someone whose demeanour is bright, healthy and cheerful, but which originally described a self-assertive person, proud and of upright bearing: as Edmund Spenser wrote in *The Shepheards Calendar* (1579): 'They wont in the wind wagge their wrigle tailes, perke as a peacock.'

**Person** The legal euphemism for a man's penis, and therefore also the police and occasionally polite name. A man accused of indecent exposure is said in court to have 'indecently exposed his person to insult any female'. Person is also a useful prefix or suffix word now obligatory in order to avoid sexist uses of the word 'man' – or, more rarely, 'woman'. It is illegal to advertise for a GIRL FRIDAY, a Handyman, Handmaiden (see AMANUENSIS), Postman or Dinner Lady (the latter, however, are always 'ladies', unlike Women Teachers). See also CHAIR and WIMMIN.

**Persona** I am at a loss to understand the attraction this word holds for some people when they really mean either 'person' or 'personality'.

**Pest control officer** See RODENT OPERATIVE.

**Photogs** See JOURNOS.

**Pig meat**  The new EURO jargon word for pork. Even plain beef and mutton are now 'beef meat' and 'sheep meat', respectively. Gone are the nice old distinctions between meat on the hoof against meat on the butcher's slab. The explanation we were given at school was that after the conquest of England the Norman masters only saw the meat on the table, and called it by the French names (*porc, boeuf*, etc.) but the conquered English yokels continued to use English names for the animals they tended in the fields but seldom ate. A pretty theory, but one that falls down on *agneau* – lamb – unless the Normans made a habit of eating Englishmen called Agnew.

**Pillar(s) of society**  This cliché description of the alleged social worth and standing of a person or persons is a translation of *Samfundets Stotter* by Henrik Ibsen (1828–1906). The play, which first appeared in 1877, was produced in London on 15 December 1880 at the Gaiety Theatre (the first Ibsen drama to be staged in England) in a translation by William Archer, but under the title *Quicksands*, which was only later changed to *Pillars of Society*. This is also its German title, *Stützen der Gesellschaft*, and indeed has given rise to the same kind of cliché-term in that language.

**Pillow talk**  Intimate, amorous or salacious conversations held in bed between lovers or a husband and his wife. But in its commercial, industrial and espionage meanings, the talk the couples engage in is thought to concern not sex but company or state secrets.

**Pinko**  American word for a person with communist or SOCIALIST sympathies, or a FELLOW-TRAVELLER. See also -NIK and -O.

**(The) pits**  A term of abuse ('Referee, you're the pits!') popularised in Britain from the early 1980s by the outbursts of John McEnroe, an American tennis player. It is thought that his pits referred to sweaty armpits, which is something tennis players are presumably familiar with. But a not unrelated ancient SCOUSE expression for things or feelings that are unpleasant is 'under de arm' (as in 'That telly programme wuz a bit under de arm'), with a stronger variant, 'under de crutch'. A Liverpudlian might visit his doctor and say, without the least facetiousness, 'Doctor, I'm really feelin' under de crutch today.' The arts critics of Liverpool newspapers occasionally describe plays, entertainments and other public events as having been 'under the arm', without the need for further explanations to their readers. (See *Lern Yerself Scouse*, Scouse Press.)

**Plastic**  As in 'Woolworths go Plastic': a credit card. See also FLEXIBLE FRIEND.

**Please print**  An injunction found on many forms, both official and private, meaning 'please write in capital letters'. The confusion is widespread and old. ' "Mr Weller . . . here's a letter for you . . ." "It can't be from the gov'ner," said Sam, looking at the direction . . . "He prints, I know, 'cos he learnt writin' from the large bills in the bookin' offices." ' (Charles Dickens, *The Pickwick Papers*, 1837.)

**Planner**  A kind of loose-leaf diary with many different kinds of inserts such as pockets, folders, maps, accounts forms, etc., which, although generally available for fifty years or more, has suddenly acquired cult status, especially amoung YUPPIES and other professional people. Like all such products it can be described with the desirability-suggesting prefix EXECUTIVE. See also ORGANISER.

**Plating**  Prostitutes' slang for *fellatio*, or fellating, i.e. woman-to-man oral sexual intercourse. It came to the notice of respectable people during a PAYOLA court-case in the mid-1970s, when a judge asked, 'What is plating?' and received a full and exact definition from the woman-witness who had used the word. Grose's *Dictionary of the Vulgar Tongue* (1811) has 'to be in for the plate', which he says means 'to be venereally infected'. Other authorities have suggested some connection with a dental plate, though this seems implausible. Perhaps the word was coined inadvertently by someone trying to say 'fellating' with the mouth full, i.e. the Love that *cannot* speak its Name.

**Ploughman's lunch**  One of the sillier manifestations of English PUB GRUB, dating from the late 1960s, although the OED Supplement records a passage dating from 1837 in which there figures a poet who had 'an extemporized sandwich, that looked like a ploughman's luncheon, in his hand'. Today's 'ploughman' (as barmaids and waiters snappily describe it) consists of bread and cheese garnished with pickles and consumed with a glass of beer. But there are many variations. Some establishments offer what they call an 'Executive Ploughman's Lunch', some – afraid of accusations of sexism – a 'Ploughperson's Lunch'; and there are other extensions and (more or less facetious) references. For example, a 'Frenchman's Lunch' is thought not to involve any food at all (see FRENCH).

**Plus** Americanism meaning 'also' or 'and'. As a man interviewed on television said, 'He's disadvantaged because he's black. Plus he is gay ...' or a well-known broadcaster: 'Today we deal with unmarried mothers plus we bring you the latest news on ...'

**Poke** See TUT.

**Police brutality** A war-cry of the extreme LEFT. Although the British police force must, by the laws of average, include members who are brutal, cruel, sadistic bullies, and although there are known to have been instances of innocent (as well as not-so-innocent) people getting beaten up, even murdered, by 'bobbies', the British policeman is still the calmest and most humane in the world. Many English blacks would disagree with this, and more of them experience the rough end of the 'law' than whites. But anyone who disagrees with the general sentiment expressed in this paragraph is invited to try upsetting an American, Russian, French, German, Austrian, Belgian, Italian, Spanish or Portuguese policeman at close quarters – let alone one in the West Indies or Africa. See also OVER-POLICING.

**Political animal** A common description – more often a slightly apologetic self-description ('I'm a political animal') – of someone who is interested in politics. It is often said, but who said it for the first time? You don't hear 'I'm a musical/artistic/sexual/sensual/ etc. animal.'

**Political poodles** The lap-dog analogy was first made by David Lloyd George on 26 June 1907, in reply to a Conservative MP who had described the House of Lords as 'the watchdog of the Constitution'. Lloyd George (apparently forgetting the ancient custom of addressing the Speaker, or CHAIR) said, 'You mean it is

Mr Balfour's poodle. It fetches and carries for him. It barks for him. It bites anyone that he sets it on to.' See also MONKEYS and WATCHDOGS.

**Political wing** If there were a burglars' trade association, its members, although individually pursued by the law, would be entitled to open offices with a brass plate on the door proclaiming themselves *The Amalgamated British Union of Burglars, Housebreakers and Associated Trades – Political Wing.* In other words, Britain is still a free country – and for many a SOFT TOUCH.

**Pornography** From the Greek words meaning 'writing about harlots' but later widened in meaning to embrace all lewd, OBSCENE or ADULT descriptions of sexual matters. The porno- prefix has in fact become a word in its own right, though it is not as fully used in its wider sense as it might be. For example, much modern rock music with its simulations of violent sexual intercourse and narcotic abandonment might be described as pornophony; and sellers of pornography could be pornopolists. The OED has pornograph, 'an obscene writing or pictorial illustration' and pornogram, 'a short pornographic poem' – which should not be confused with either a STRIPPAGRAM or a phonograph.

**Portion control** In the jargon of the catering and food industry, a euphemism for giving the customer as little to eat as possible for as high a price as may decently be charged.

**Positive** Favourable, not NEGATIVE. Positive feelings good, negative feelings bad. Positive discrimination is the – often necessary – remedy for getting DISADVANTAGED minorities recognised, given homes, employment, etc.

**Postal delayers** Although the British Post Office denies their existence, there are men and women in its employ whose job it is to sort second-class mail from first-class. Whatever they are called, the purpose of their action is to make sure second-class letters are not inadvertently delivered too quickly.

**Postgraduate** An *adjective* describing a student who has graduated from a university or similar establishment of higher education, i.e. has taken a degree, but then embarks on

postgraduate studies. It is not a noun, and the only person who
could logically describe himself as 'a postgraduate' would be a
dead graduate.

**(The) pound in your pocket**  One of many memorably effective
political utterances that often return to haunt those who made
them. In a broadcast on 20 November 1967 the then Prime Minister,
Mr Harold (now Lord) Wilson, announcing the devaluation of the
pound, reassured the nation in these words: 'It does not mean, of
course, that the pound here in Britain in your pocket or purse or
in your bank has been devalued.' In the sense in which he meant
it, the statement was true. But before long the international oil
crisis ensured that Britain suffered record inflation, and the pound
was decimalised into the ridiculous PEE, a process which some
say was designed not so much to HARMONISE with Europe but in
order to disguise the fact that Britons were soon to pay twelve
shillings for a loaf of bread and nearly four shillings to post a
letter. By 1967 standards the 1987 pound in our pocket is worth
less than a shilling.

**(The) powers that be**  Now used loosely (some say too widely)
to denote any kind of authority, from the headmaster to the village
constable, from the government to the local planning-officer,
usually as a cliché. But it comes from a most respectable source –
St Paul's Epistle to the Romans (13.1): 'Let every soul be in
subjection to the higher powers: for there is no power but of
God; and the powers that be are ordained of God.'

**Pragmatism**  See U-TURN.

**Preused**  (Sometimes pre-used but surely to be preferred in the
suitably ugly one-word version) A euphemism for second-hand,
as in 'a preused car'. Imported from America. See also WOULD YOU
BUY A USED CAR ...?

**(The) ... process**  As in 'the decision-making process', the 'peace
process', 'the conciliation process', etc. A German-based
Americanism adopted into British English used to describe
something that is ONGOING. So American is it that even Englishmen
sometimes say it with an American accent, i.e. not 'proe-cess' but
'praw-cess'.

**Propaganda** From the Latin, *Congregatio de propaganda fide*, a 'College for Propagating the Faith' which was first proposed by Pope Gregory XIII but not put into effect until 1622 by Gregory XV. The college emphasised the need for the faithful to propagate the Catholic religion to unbelievers throughout the world, and was therefore a sort of society of missionaries, thenceforth colloquially known in English as 'the Propaganda'. It remained a religious term until the French stirrings of revolutionary fervour gave the word a political meaning – one which has now totally supplanted the original sense. (And 'propaganda' is not, as some claim, a plural falsely treated as singular, like agenda, data and MEDIA, etc.) The first (communist) propagandists in their revolutionary fervour modelled themselves on the religious missionaries. As the *Gentleman's Magazine* explained in 1790, 'The Propaganda (is) a society whose members are bound, by solemn engagements, to stir up subjects against their lawful rulers.' In spite of all this, and all the manifold subsequent developments for which see DISINFORMATION, PSYCHOLOGICAL WARFARE, Rome still remembers the original propagandists, with a road called *Via Propaganda*, near St Peter's. The essence of spreading political propaganda lies in the ceaseless repetition of platitudes turned into SLOGANS, as practised, to give a recent notable example, by MILITANT.

**Property-owning democracy** A term much in the news after the Conservatives embarked on a successful process of cheaply selling council houses to their occupiers, thus increasing at a stroke the number of CAPITALISTS in Britain. It was believed to be an aspect of THATCHERISM but is in fact far older. The idea was first propounded in a book entitled *Constructive Conservatism* by A. Skelton (1924), and the term used in a speech by Sir Anthony Eden at the Conservative Party Conference in October 1946. 'Until our educated and politically-minded democracy has become predominantly a property-owning democracy, neither the national equilibrium nor the balance of the life of the individual will be restored.' The sale of nationalised industries to millions of small shareholders drawn from ordinary people who would previously never have risked money on the stock-exchange (and who, some said, had owned the industries in the first place) was an extension of the same process. It cleverly ensured that renationalisation (i.e. dispossession) by a future Labour government would be almost impossible.

**Protection** Since around 1860 the shortened euphemistic name for Protection Racket, i.e. a form of extortion and BLACKMAIL by which money is demanded from shopkeepers and others in return for alleged protection against molestation by others. In practice the 'others' are in fact the same persons as the extortioners. Protection rackets are learnt early, and in many INNER CITY areas small children lie in wait for car-owners about to park their vehicles and cry, 'Can I mind yer car, mister?' The resulting ransom is extorted against an implied threat of damage to the car if it is refused.

**Psychiatric hospital** In Russia and other communist countries (at any rate until the Gorbachev era of GLASNOST brought signs of hope), this is a euphemism for a prison where DISSIDENTS are BRAINWASHED. The American poet Emily Dickinson (1830–1886) anticipated the idea:

> Much madness is divinest sense to a discerning Eye,
>     Much sense, the starkest Madness.
> Assent – and you are sane;
>     Demur – you're straightway dangerous
> And handled with a Chain.

**Psychological warfare** The use of PROPAGANDA to undermine, unsettle or discomfit an enemy, generally by means of DISINFORMATION. During the Second World War the British had a highly effective psychological warfare department, run with the help of distinguished academics as well as German and Austrian Jewish refugees who had an insight and knowledge of both the mind and the language of the enemy. The Germans' efforts were much cruder, not much different from those used during the First World War, consisting largely of leaflets (often in faulty English) telling the 'Tommies' that their wives were being unfaithful, or playing on front-line loudspeakers or on the radio records of *Lilli Marlene* so as to make them feel homesick(!). As an unintended result this sickly and MAUDLIN song achieved an immediate popularity in Britain, which to some extent it still enjoys.

**Pub grub** A sign often seen outside English inns since the late 1960s, when many innkeepers began to realise that their establishments could be made more attractive if they offered more than merely alcoholic drinks. It is perhaps characteristic of the widespread take-it-or-leave-it attitude that the unappetising if rhyming (and possibly ambiguous) word 'grub' was preferred to 'food'. Before the 1960s and early 70s it was often difficult to obtain so much as a sandwich in an English pub. Some customers were even obliged to invoke an ancient law that compels innkeepers to provide food and shelter to travellers. Pub grub now generally consists of uncooked or cold food, like the ubiquitous PLOUGHMAN'S LUNCH, a cold sausage, or green salads – with or without 'grubs' – though some pubs offer what is jocularly described as 'home cooking'.

**Public school** In the English educational system, a private school.

**Pull-out supplement** Euphemism for what is usually a throw-away, an advertising feature or SPECIAL REPORT inserted in a newspaper or magazine in order to attract advertising revenue. See also PERKS, FREEBIES and their cross-references.

**Pulp-** The literary equivalent of the JUNK- prefix, that is, trashy, ephemeral, low-quality books and magazines which are printed on cheap paper and (by implication) will soon revert to waste-paper by being repulped. One might suppose that the word would have come into use only after the Second World War, when the re-use of paper became general practice, but the OED has a recorded reference to 'the pulps' dated 1931. In the magazine trade the opposite of pulps are the GLOSSIES.

**Punk** An old word that came back into fashion during the late 1970s and early 80s, although with a new meaning. The new punks follow a nihilistic cult of ugliness, with aggressive behaviour that manifests itself in a sort of hairstyle, tattoos and dress; also in a kind of quasi-musical performance featuring crude noisiness and lack of skill, any pretence of singing is abandoned in favour of rhythmic screaming and shouting. The dress associated with the cult arrogantly flaunts ugliness and dirt, Nazi emblems, and metal-studded leather. Punks are still sometimes seen in cities but derided or dismissed as exhibitionists (a derision in which they pretend to revel). A large number of punk 'musicians' slid into narcotic crimes and even murder, which caused the fashion to decline, though in some circles it still commands a small but fanatical following. For a short time the punk movement was politicised by LEFTists as well as fascists, who both claimed it for their own as 'an expression of the despair of underprivileged youth' – and similar pretentious rot. When Shakespeare used the word (e.g. in *Measure for Measure*, V.1. 179) he meant a prostitute: 'She may be a Puncke: for many of them are neither Maid, Widow nor Wife . . .' The OED thinks punk may be connected with punch and puncture, as well as spunk, the dysphemism for sperm. Other meanings given include a Chinese joss-stick, and a kind of wood used for tinder. The OED also has the adjective punky, like a punk; and, rather charmingly, punklet, a small or young punk. During the 1920s the word was banned in America by the Hays Office controlling morals in the film industry – together with BROAD, floozy, harlot, hussy, madam, slut, trollop, tart, prostitute, hot mamma and wench!

**Punter**  A hideous and rather contemptuous new name for a customer, especially fashionable among JOURNALISTS who like to interject colloquialisms into their prose, e.g. 'downing bubbly' for drinking champagne, etc. They borrow the word from prostitutes, who use it when referring to their clients. A punter was originally one who gambled or took risks, so the HOOKERS' usage is certainly more apt than the HACKS'. People who gamble their money on the football pools also call themselves punters, although the pools promoters prefer grandly to describe them as 'investors': a nice euphemism, since an investor is one who expects, and nearly always gets, some return on his investment, whereas football punters know they are extremely unlikely ever to see a penny of their gambling outlay back. But what kind of inference is one to draw from the Irish government's decision to describe its monetary unit, formerly the simple British pound, as a punt?

**Putsch**  It is appropriate that when Englishmen speak about the violent overthrow of lawful governments, or attempts to do so, they prefer to borrow words from foreigners, who know more about such events. But, surprisingly, *Putsch* is a dialect word which emanates from the peaceful Swiss cantons, where it means a knock, a thrust or a blow, exactly the same as the French word *coup*. Did the Swiss ever have occasion to use the word in the revolutionary sense? Now that British protesters have perfected the DEMO to a fine and often bloody art (and some elected MPs openly advise people to 'take to the streets when recourse to parliament fails') they may as well use their own, indigenous words. Revolt, uprising and revolution seem to cover the subject perfectly adequately. The use of *Putsch* has in any case much abated since the defeat of Nazi Germany (the Russians don't seem to permit a word of that meaning to enter general usage) and news items announcing that there had been 'a coup in Peru' may not be taken very seriously. The OED dates the first use of *Putsch* at 3 June 1920, when *The Times* considered the possibility of a *Putsch* in Germany (giving the word a capital initial letter, as all German nouns should be given, and putting it in italics). But the now largely forgotten words Putschist and Putschism appeared in English in 1898: 'Putschism is the fanatical tendency towards street struggle, faith in the barricades.' The elected MP referred to above is clearly a putschist.

# Q

**Queens' English** See RENT BOY.

**Quisling** One of many 1939–1945 war-words which have gone out of use, like FRATTING. When the war ended the reckoning began for those who had collaborated with the German invaders, and they were branded as either collaborators or collaborationists. The Norwegian traitor Vidkun Quisling, however, gave his name to the species.

**Quite** An all-purpose sort of word which can mean 'completely, entirely, wholly', as in 'I have quite finished'; or be used sarcastically, as in 'Have you quite finished?'; or mean 'partly' or 'a little', as in 'She is *quite* pretty'. And 'quite' (short for 'quite so') is a way of saying 'yes, I agree'. The word became fashionable during the last quarter of the 19th century, and was singled out by *Punch* for a satirical cartoon (see opposite).

## REFINEMENTS OF MODERN SPEECH.

*Female Exquisite.* " QUITE A NICE BALL AT MRS. MILLEFLEURS', WASN'T IT ? "
*Male Ditto.* " VERY QUITE.  INDEED, REALLY *MOST* QUITE ! "

*Punch, 7th February 1874*

# R

**Racism** In the sense in which it is now on everyone's lips, this word is to 'racialism' what 'oriented' is to 'orientated' – that is, a malapropism which has become accepted and legitimised to such a degree that anyone who now uses the correct form is likely to be 'corrected', or at any rate may get funny looks. *Racialism*, says the OED, is a belief in the superiority of a particular race leading to prejudice and antagonism towards people of other races, especially those in close proximity who may be felt as a threat to one's cultural and racial integrity or economic well-being. And that, of course, is an abomination. *Racism,* on the other hand, is the theory that distinctive human characteristics and abilities are *determined* by race. No-one can generalise about 'abilities', for these are difficult to categorise; but differences in 'human characteristics' are indisputable, namely that Afro-Caribbeans are likely to have darker skin than Sino-Japanese, who may have narrower eyes than Celts, who are of smaller average height than people of Norse descent, who are predominantly fairer-haired than Jews, who tend to have thinner, longer noses than Afro-Caribbeans. So much for neutral characteristics. On the positive side, it has been shown that Afro-Caribbean black children in English schools tend to be better at sports than Asian or European ones. And where racial misfortunes are concerned, a leaflet I picked up in my doctor's surgery says 'Sickle cell anaemia occurs almost exclusively in black people'; and I read elsewhere that some other disease afflicts chiefly Semites, i.e. Jews and Arabs. In addition, I would guess that the three-and-a-half thousand years' continuous tradition of universal literacy of the Jews (and to a less universal extent the Chinese) may have exerted some racist-hereditary influence, e.g. a respect for books and a capacity for book-learning. The two words, racism and racialism, have been confused since the 1930s, when Hitler's racialist policies were much discussed and written about in this country; but in recent years, for reasons that need hardly be stated, the confusion has been worse confounded and much compounded. Another frequent confusion lies in the fact that colour-prejudice, for which there can be no excuse, is often interpreted as, or confused with, culture-prejudice, which is legitimate and understandable. Although the British, with their

bad colonialist record and worse conscience, suffer much abuse
for alleged racialism, they must never cease pointing out that the
worst sorts of ethnic and racialist discrimination, intolerance and
violence occur between smaller groups of their former colonial
subjects like the Tamils, Hindus, Muslims and countless other
national, religious or ethnic sects, as well as all the warring Arab
FACTIONS and constant tribal warfare in Africa.

**Radical** A word whose meaning changes with prevailing
political and/or social or other conditions, with the locality it is
(over-)used in, or by those who use it. It comes from the Latin
word for a root, *radix*, and also has ancient botanical and
philosophical meanings. But today, when you read in a
newspaper, 'It would be hard to imagine a more alternative
lawyer than ****. He and his wife, a radical midwife ...' you know
exactly what is meant by ALTERNATIVE but not by 'radical'. A
'radical' lawyer today is not necessarily a solicitor or barrister
who has a deep-rooted grounding in the law – though he may
have – but one who specialises in the defence of members of
ETHNIC minorities, of alleged offenders against civil order, rioters,
the 'Angry' BRIGADE of yesteryear, and those accused of an offence
they hold to have been political. It is often interesting to speculate
about their motives for such legal specialisation. Some are
themselves active in radical politics, or are of the same national
origin as their clients, which gives them a natural understanding,
but others do so simply because, when times are hard, it pays to
specialise, and to become well known as a specialist, in a field
where there is a great deal of work. On the other hand, ****'s
spouse, the 'radical midwife', might be merely a lady of the
extreme political LEFT (now the most common meaning of
'radical') or she may advocate some unspecified 'radical' form of
childbirth – about which there is also much current discussion but
which fortunately does not fall within the province or interest of
this book. Bearing in mind the original Latin word *radix*, radical
childbirth sounds more uncomfortable for the mother than the
midwife.

**Radiogram** An old-fashioned music CENTRE, dating from the last
days of the WIRELESS, before this was popularly renamed 'the
radio'.

**-rama** American suffix of commerce and trade, as in launderama, shopperama, barberama, etc. See also -ORIUM, -TERIA.

**Rap** At first (since the 18th century) a rebuke or reprimand ('taking the rap'); then an American colloquial word for talks or discussions; then, transferred, as 'rap clubs', establishments where sexual intercourse in various forms is sold under the guise of being places for informal 'chats' (like 'massage parlours', 'SAUNA clubs' etc.) From this came another current meaning: 'singing' tunelessly (actually, rhythmic shouting in a deadpan manner and without any vocal or musical inflexion whatever) with or without drum and/or guitar accompaniment, generally by Blacks. The text is usually one with a 'social' message and occasionally inflammatory.

**Rationalisation** Commercial and fiscal euphemism for reducing services while at the same time probably increasing costs. Firms engage in rationalisation by putting their own convenience and profit before service to the customer, or reducing the range of products. 'There is no call for it' usually means 'We can't be bothered to stock it, and besides, profits aren't big enough to make it worth while.' In the National Health Service rationalisation means closing the smaller hospitals and replacing them with a single, huge, central establishment many miles away, which not only takes more people and more money to run but also costs lives because emergency cases have greater distances to travel.

**Reactionary** In its earliest application, from about 1840, one who is held to be in opposition to a revolution; but later a term of abuse applied by LEFT-wing persons to each other – seldom to persons of the RIGHT. When political theorists of certain persuasions start arguing, this word is always among the first to be bandied about.

**Real** As in Real Ale, Real Bread, etc. A product of the WHOLE food movement, but the Campaign for Real Ale (CAMRA – one of the earliest trendy acronyms of its kind) can claim to have started the fashion. There is also a hint of the American kind of real, i.e. used in place of really, e.g. real sick, real good, real mad, etc.

**Recharging (my) batteries** Euphemistic excuse for having a holiday, e.g. a BREAK, which, the speaker feels, others may think he does not really deserve. Also FREE-LOADING and UNWINDING.

**Redundant** In older usage an adjective meaning unnecessary, superfluous; but since the great wave of unemployment hit Britain in the early 1970s, 'being made redundant' is heard with melancholy frequency. It is only a politer, softened, euphemism for the more brutal 'getting the sack' (itself a colloquialism long considered standard English). But to be *made* redundant is different from *becoming* redundant (not unlike the difference between disappearing and *going* (!) missing. See also CONSULTANCY.

**Refusenik** A Russian (usually but not necessarily a Jew) who has been refused permission to emigrate. See -NIK.

**Regional** Euphemism for 'provincial'. The OED defines the latter as '. . . exhibiting the character, especially the narrowness of view or interest, associated with or attributed to inhabitants of ''the provinces''; wanting the culture or polish of the capital'. No wonder the BBC, for one, soon decided to refer to its provincial centres as 'the regions'; and so do politicians – when they remember.

**(The) regions** The provinces (see above and FOGEY).

**Rent-a-** Said by some to be the invention of Hertz Rent-a-Car. But a correspondent to the OED found a company called Rent-a-Ford which was active in the United States as early as 1921. Extended into any number of sardonic applications, and much used by the RIGHT to describe DEMOS organised by the LEFT. Peter Simple wrote in the *Daily Telegraph* in December 1961: 'Dictators!!! When you liberate a territory or mop up a colonialist enclave, are you disappointed and upset to receive only a tepid welcome from the people? Let *rentacrowd* help you.' Three years later Christopher Driver in his book *The Disarmers* wrote of 'the phenomenon Peter Simple ... cruelly christened ''Rentacrowd'': London's instantly available progressive claque ready ... to demonstrate on a whole range of causes'. Since then the rent-a-SYNDROME has come a long way. And is not necessarily always a political phenomenon. Pop singers' publicity agents can always be relied on to arrange for their temporary idol a suitably hysterical welcome from the gullible young. During the

prolonged miners' strike of the 1980s the term Flying Pickets
joined Rent-a-Crowd.

**Rent boy**  A male prostitute. Since the AIDS scare of the late 1980s,
a disease which, in spite of widespread propaganda to the
contrary, then affected mostly homosexual men and drugs
misusers, the term has entered the language to such an extent
that newspapers employ it without explanation or even isolating
it in quotation-marks. So have several other specialist terms
belonging to what is often called 'queens' English'. Many are
ingenious and scandalously witty and many more quite
disgusting. They can be found in *Gay Talk* by Bruce Rogers
(Paragon Books).

**Rescheduling (debts)**  Euphemism for the postponement of the
repayment of national debts, which, in the case of the THIRD WORLD,
usually means indefinitely.

**Researcher**  In the dissembling world of television production
the TALKING HEAD seen on the screen is seldom responsible for the
words it utters. As the credits roll, the names of otherwise unsung
researchers or GHOSTS briefly appear and disappear, people who
may have worked for weeks and months to assemble the facts and
formulate words to put on to the autocue and into the mouth of
the presenter. It is he or she who gets the biggest credit – and is
considered by the watching public to be a great expert on the
subject. The resulting book, if one is PACKAGED, will carry his name
printed large on the cover, and the researchers' names
somewhere inside, very small – if they are lucky. They will
probably work on a fixed contract fee, whereas the presenter
reaps the royalties. However, in one embarrassing case, the
researchers subsequently sued the television presenter who had
wrongly taken all the credit and were handsomely rewarded both
with acknowledgments of their efforts and the royalties they
deserved. See also GHOST.

**Residential home**  An apparent tautology: what else is a home
where one resides but residential? But it is in fact a modern
euphemism for what used to be called a 'work house': also a
curious term, as it was the home where people went when they
were no longer able to work or support themselves. See also
SENIOR CITIZEN and SUNSET HOME.

**Resource** 'A means of supplying some want or deficiency; a stock or reserve upon which one can draw when necessary. Now usually *plural*'. Since the OED printed that definition, 'resource', both as verb and noun, has acquired the status of a BUZZ WORD in social and educational jargon, often in conjunction with CENTRE. To be 'insufficiently resourced' now means to be lacking in something, usually the things money can buy. It works well with almost any combination of other buzz words. For example, when the LOONY Liverpool City Council founded a very laudable and worth-while organisation for helping the unemployed it named it 'The Merseyside Trade Union COMMUNITY and Unemployed Resource Centre' – one of whose 'resources', incidentally, is a licensed bar called the 'Flying Picket' (See RENT-A-).

**Revanchism** A word to conjure with after the First World War, and generally applied to German politicians eager to gain revenge for the alleged indignities inflicted on their country after its defeat by the allies. Occasionally and derogatorily said of Israeli HAWKS who advocate state retaliation against Arab terrorists – see FIGHTER.

**Reverse discrimination** See POSITIVE discrimination.

**Revisionism** A theory of communist revolution-by-evolution advocated in the 1890s (i.e. before the Russian Revolution) by Edward Bernstein, who was, however, shouted down by the revolutionaries, who made revisionism a dirty word. See also REACTIONARY, DEVIATIONISM and other cross-references to words the Soviets use to describe those who are thought to be BOLSHY about the currently approved brand of Russian communist doctrine.

**Richard Roe** See JOHN DOE.

**Riding** For nearly 1000 years, until the useless, bureaucracy-ridden and highly unpopular reorganisation of the English counties took place in the early 1970s, the Ridings were the three counties that comprised Yorkshire – East Riding, West Riding and North Riding (*South Riding* is fictitious, a novel by Winifred Holtby). Contrary to popular supposition, riding in this sense has nothing to do with riding on horseback, nor (as some have suggested) a certain distance measured in relation to the time it

takes to complete it on horseback. The original word was
'thriding', i.e. 'thirding', Old English for a third part.

**Right**[1] See LEFT.

**Right**[2] Interjection of American origin (where it was translated
from a common German conversational tic). When said by the
speaking partner in a conversation it has a questioning inflexion
(*Right?*), gets a great deal of emphasis (*Right?*), and is interpolated
at maddeningly frequent intervals (*Right?*) as though the speaker
needed reassurance that he was talking sense (*Right?*). The
passive, listening partner, on the other hand, murmurs *Right!*
rather more calmly and quietly, to pronounce assent. Such habits
are more common in some circles than others – usually the trendy
LEFT. (*Right?*)

**Rights movement** Not far removed from the protest movement,
but rooted in the often courageous stand made by American
liberals to obtain equal rights for Blacks. In Northern Ireland a
movement with the same name campaigned, often violently, for
the rights of the Roman Catholic minority.

**Rock opera** A pretentious euphemism for an allegedly musical
play (play?) distinguished (distinguished?) by raucous singing
(singing?) and loud drumming. It has as much to do with opera as
ROCK SALMON has with salmon.

**Rock salmon** Fishmongers' euphemism for dog-fish which, for
obvious reasons, is unlikely to appeal to the British as a delicacy.

**Rodent operative** Euphemism for what used to be a rat-catcher.
Those OPERATIVES whose brief is wider than killing just rats and
mice also work under the name of Pest Control Officers.

**Rumpus** Used mostly by journalists when they want to
exaggerate or sensationalise some slight disturbance. The OED
says it is 'probably a fanciful formation', therefore no Latin origin
seems likely, in spite of the -us ending. Rumpus-room is an
American coinage of about 1940 and is a room set aside for
recreation and enjoyment, i.e. of indoor sports, hobbies, etc.,
and which does not need to be kept tidy.

**Russian roulette** Considering the cool relations that have existed between Russia and the West for the greater part of this century I am surprised how few NEGATIVE terms are prefixed by that country's name, certainly compared with what the French and the Dutch have had to suffer in the way of irrational verbal abuse, from the French Pox to the Dutch Treat. But what is the origin  of the allegedly Russian method of suicide-by-gambling, when the barrel of a revolver is spun, the gun held to the head and the trigger pulled, in the hope that the barrel might have come to rest at an empty chamber? Apart from this piece of lethal bravado, there is the game of Russian Rumour, in which messages are whispered from person to person so that some comically garbled form might emerge at the end of the line. Perhaps with GLASNOST the joke is on its way out. (Another name for this game is Chinese Whispers.) See also VATICAN ROULETTE.

# S

**Sanitary warden** Euphemistic official title for what used to be known as a Lavatory Attendant.

**Sanitised** Literally, made healthy, disinfected. But often used figuratively to describe a cleaned-up image or something made to appear respectable, at least outwardly, like the LAUNDERING of money.

**Sauna parlour** No doubt there are many genuine establishments that offer their customers the pleasant and ancient Scandinavian combination of dry heat with alternating douches of cold water, followed perhaps by genuine, expert body-massage. But very often 'Sauna/Massage' is a euphemism for providing various sexual services in return for payment. In this way sauna and massage are the 20th-century successors of the stews and bagnios – understandably so, since such recreations are taken while the participants are naked. Other more or less thinly disguised verbal euphemisms for prostitution include 'French Lessons' (a curious throwback to Victorian days, when the word FRENCH was held to hold endless promise of naughtiness and vice), 'Strict Disciplinarian' or 'Corrective Treatment' (services for masochists) and 'Escort Services'. 'Models', too, may be suspect – much to the chagrin of real models, whether fashion, artists' or photographic. Genuine 'male models', too, are always at pains to stress that they follow an honourable calling.

**Scientist** One of the great words of contention in the 19th century. Farmer's *Dictionary of Americanisms* in 1889 wrote: 'A man of science. In the commencement of the philological battle concerning the termination "ist," the thick of the fight was mainly waged round this word, it being one of the earliest introductions of the class. Compared with some recent forms (see FRUITIST) [Farmer's injunction but see also FRUITIST in this book!] *scientist* is a highly respectable, working member of [the] Society of Uncouth Words and Phrases.' See also JOURNALISM.

**Scouse** The dialect spoken in Liverpool and the Merseyside area; a Scouser is therefore a Liverpudlian, although there is no residential or birth qualification like that which requires of a Cockney to be born within the sound of Bow Bells. It is not merely an accent, i.e. normal English spoken with a different pronunciation, but a dialect, having a vocabulary markedly different from standard English (see *Lern Yerself Scouse, or How to talk proper on Merseyside*, by Shaw, Spiegl and Kelly, Scouse Press, Liverpool, 1964 onwards). Scouse is an abbreviation of Lobscouse, itself an anglicised form of *Labskaus*, which is a North German seafarers' dish, poor man's food not unlike Irish Stew. The OED defines Lobscouse as 'a sailors' dish of meat stewed with vegetables and ship's biscuit or the like' and a lobscouser as 'a sailor, a tar'. The German *Brockhaus* dictionary, on the other hand, says *Labskaus* is 'a Norwegian sailor's dish of salt beef or fish, with mashed potatoes'; and a German cookery-book about 120 years old gives the following recipe:

Boil a piece of fairly lean salt-beef (or equal quantities of beef and ham) till soft, and chop it into coarse pieces. Meanwhile boil some potatoes in unsalted water and add a great quantity of small onions which have been braised in butter. Mash all this together, season with pepper and pour over it enough of the meat stock to produce a mash of soft consistency. This simple dish is extremely nourishing when taken with pickled cucumber or a glass of beer.

*Labe* is German for a refreshing comfort, e,g. welcome food or drink taken by a hungry man, and *labberig* as something that is insipid and soft, like mashed potatoes. All in all, the recipe is one of many variations of Irish stew which, like Scouse, is traditionally eaten with pickled red cabbaqe. In the poorer circles of Liverpool there used also to be, in the old days of depression before the WELFARE STATE, an even simpler variation called Blind Scouse, which has all the ingredients above except for the meat, which is substituted perhaps by gravy left over from a previous meal.

**Scribes**  See JOURNOS.

**Second world**  See THIRD WORLD.

**Selected**  As in 'selected carrots', or even 'specially selected': a usually meaningless commercial description of goods. Selected for what?

**Self-starters**  See HEAD-HUNTING and MOTIVATION.

**Seminar**  The EXECUTIVE businessman's preferred word for a business meeting, or conference. The word comes from the Latin *semen*, meaning 'seed', and seminars are indeed meant to be occasions for sowing the seeds of knowledge, e.g. sales conferences held with the avowed aim of making better salesmen, though these meetings may also involve the sowing of wild oats. There is, however, probably less actual *conferring* at such conferences and rather more listening to speeches and lectures. But the immediate modern origin of the seminar seems to lie in the American (from the German) usage of the word for a study group, usually at a university. Conferences (a practice also copied from America) are now so popular that many cities have built special and lavishly-appointed conference CENTRES. Medical people are fond of holding their conferences (often subsidised by one or more pharmaceutical companies) in exotic, far-flung places, where the sun is always shining, and exchange their knowledge and research between entertainments and sight-seeing trips; and many of the big multinationals use them as a thinly-disguised way of rewarding their more successful salesmen with holidays abroad. But it is the word symposium that gives the game away. It is Greek for a drinking-party, 'a convivial meeting for drinking, conversation and intellectual entertainment', says the OED (and in that order!). The conversazione must also be included here, although it is altogether a more refined kind of meeting: in Italy, from the early 18th century, it meant 'an evening assembly for conversation, social recreation and amusement'. But by the end of the 18th century it was a meeting of 'a learned body or society of arts at which (its) work is illustrated by the exhibition of specimens, experiments, etc'. Even more lofty are the annual meetings of SYNOD.

**Senior citizen**   WELFARE-STATE word for an old-age pensioner. As the years go by I find this euphemism less offensive, but not the prospect of living in a SUNSET HOME, or even a RESIDENTIAL HOME in a TWILIGHT AREA. Or of being labelled a pensioner when one is not in receipt of a pension.

**Separatists**   Subversive foreigners in search of political and military power, which they hope to achieve by breaking away from the rest of their people, from whom they feel separated by different language, customs and tradition, etc. In this they are at variance with the general trend of respectable politics, which has always striven towards strength through unity, e.g. the United States, the Union of Soviet Socialist Republics and now the European Community. Like other LIBERATION FRONTS, the size and organisational strength of separatists is usually in inverse proportion to the havoc they are able to inflict on innocent civilians. Most of them, no doubt, consist of a mere handful of small groups in possession of a CACHE of weapons and explosives (supplied, perhaps, by one of the SUPER-powers anxious to widen their spheres of influence in far-away places). See also FUNDAMENTALISTS.

**Seventh heaven**   A place of extreme happiness. See also CLOUD NINE and OVER THE MOON, somewhere between which this heaven is believed to be situated.

**Sex'n'drugs'n'rock'n'roll**   The opening words of a notorious pop song of the 1970s beginning *Sex'n'drugs'n'rock'n'roll is all my body needs, sex'n'drugs'n'rock'n'roll is* [!] *very good indeed...',* which later became a cliché (and not only among pop-music addicts); and later still, when the drugs menace got out of control and AIDS among JUNKIES threatened to do so, a sick joke – especially as the unfortunate author of this masterpiece was obliged to make a public recantation.

**Sex typing** Nothing to do with sexual intercourse or the typing-pool but an allegedly bad educational practice which presupposes that girls are naturally interested in playing with dolls and want to learn to cook, whereas boys prefer boyish pursuits and pastimes. LOONY bodies like the Inner London Education Authority have been doing their utmost to remove these 'gender assumptions', as their unlovely jargon has it. To this end the Schools Curriculum Development Committee and the Equal Opportunities Commission in 1987 combined to issue a book entitled *Genderwatch* in which teachers of drama-classes are advised to make sure that 'the common experiences of women, such as menstruation, childbirth, childcare and SEXUAL HARASSMENT' are adequately portrayed.

**Sexual harassment** A term used by WIMMIN and others to describe any aspersion on the femaleness or femininity of women – sentiments often in direct conflict with those described in the previous entry. Sexual harassment may range from an offensively appreciative wolf-whistle or a whispered 'Hi, gorgeous!' to unwanted groping, fondling or indecent assault; or threats of loss of employment through moral blackmail of, perhaps, a secretary by her boss, with the implication 'submit to my advance or be dismissed'. Such behaviour, offensive and reprehensible among civilised people, is as old as life itself, since the male's sexual behaviour is that of the predator, and too many men unfortunately lack sensitivity and sexual manners. It is very proper that women now have the opportunity of defending themselves against these excesses, though there are inevitably instances of love-gone-wrong professional relationships that start in bed and end in court, with women amorously spurned claiming to be women legally wronged. Sadder still, for every woman who is sexually harassed there are hundreds who long for a little benevolent harassment, though WIMMIN (many of whom are undoubtedly men-hating lesbians) hotly deny this. It is also demonstrable that those who feel most strongly about sexual – or racial, or any other modern form of – harassment put the stress in 'harassment' not on the first syllable, as poets have done for centuries, but on the *ass*. This at least enables the uncommitted listener to spot immediately whether the word is being used in its neologist or traditional sense.

**Shades** Pop musicians' slang (originally American) for tinted glasses to protect the wearer's eyes from strong sunlight. But shades are worn indoors and outdoors, whether the sun is shining or not: either because the wearer has taken a certain illicit drug which makes the eyes ultra-sensitive to light, or because he or she wants to draw attention to him- or herself. Many TELEVISION PERSONALITIES famous for being famous wear sunglasses in public so that they might be recognised as someone not wishing to be recognised.

**Shelf life** A by-product of CONSUMERISM, which demands that foodstuffs bear a date by which they should be consumed. Variations on this should be recognised for the different things they imply. The shelf life of a product (which is not necessarily an edible one) is the concern of the seller, who naturally wishes to avoid having unsaleable goods left on his shelves. A 'Sell-by' date is also his concern: what the consumer decides to do with it after purchase, and when, is the consumer's own concern. 'Eat-by' is a clear instruction, after which date the product may be unfit for human consumption; but 'Best before –' leaves the decision to the consumer. These are the result of much beneficial agitation by consumerist organisations to guard us against commercial exploitation.

**Show trial** Usually applied only to a trial held in communist or other totalitarian countries, now especially African, either for the benefit of the foreign MEDIA (who are meant to be impressed by the allegedly fair and humane treatment the accused is said to be receiving) or, in another and more sinister way, for warning local residents of what might befall *them* if they step out of line. But also used figuratively and pejoratively by those subjected to a disciplinary hearing, e.g. in a trades union KANGAROO COURT or a party-political tribunal, and perhaps even by a disgruntled defendant under the English legal system who feels he should not be in the dock. This is the place to mention the two standard clichés that almost invariably issue from the lips of defendants and plaintiffs alike: 'The law is an ass' or THIS HAS RESTORED MY FAITH IN BRITISH JUSTICE, when unsuccessful or successful, respectively.

**Sick as a parrot**  An all-too-rare example of a cliché killed by satire. For years it was the stock reply of footballers, boxers and others whose primary skills lay in fields other than communicating with their fellow-men, on being asked how they felt after defeat (those who won were always 'over the moon') or suffered some other minor reverse. But eventually even they were compelled to realise how foolish the simile became with over-use. Now, whenever it is used, implied quotation-marks are usually audible.

**Simplistic**  A simplist is one who prescribes or sells herbal remedies, or simples – substances that are unmixed, uncompounded and unadulterated by others, hence 'simplistic'. But during the 1960s and 1970s, with the rise of popular television discussions, this adjective became a favourite word for scoring points with. An opponent's view would be (and often still is) dismissed as 'simplistic'. This is the meaning which has now become established, is the first meaning modern dictionaries record and must be accepted as 'correct' – especially as there are not too many herbal simplists in the National Health Service. All the more credit, therefore, to those who resist it and resort to a synonym.

**Single parent family**  A neologism coined chiefly for the laudable purpose of removing stigma from (and discrimination against) unmarried mothers, though the term may also be used by the divorced, the abandoned and the widowed, and by fathers as well as mothers.

**Sitcom**  Acronymic abbreviation of 'situation comedy', which is the mainstay of American and British television entertainment: plays with a domestic, everyday setting in which there is a minimum of plot combined with the maximum number of ONE-LINERS purporting to be smart repartee such as one seldom hears in domestic everyday settings. These are accompanied by short bursts of recorded studio laughter, characterised by the suddenness with which the sound is cut off.

**Situation** See ONGOING.

**-ski** The Russianising suffix, much used by JOURNOS. When the Russians brought out their ill-fated copy of Concorde it was immediately named 'Concordski', especially after it crashed at the first air-show it took part in.

**Skinhead** The 1957 edition of Wentworth & Flexner's *Dictionary of Americanisms* defines this as 'a bald man', but the Supplement published ten years later adds, 'A man with a shaved head or a closely-cropped head of hair' and also, 'A Marine recruit', doubtless because the first thing he got was an exaggeratedly short haircut (as happens to recruits the world over – except in Holland, where the armed forces apparently encourage long hair). Soon afterwards the British skinhead came on the scene: 'A youth (often one of a gang), also typically characterised by wearing workman-like clothing and heavy boots, and by a tendency to aggressive behaviour' (OED). These 'workman-like clothes' may take the form of boiler-suits, or a variety of leather garb studded with metal objects and chains worn in various places thereon but there are subdivisions and cult-variations unlikely to interest readers of this book. The apparent liking of these PUNK-like rebels for uniform and short, often shaved, head-hair, does not indicate a propensity towards discipline such as might be found in the armed forces. On the contrary, skinheads and their various associates are politically and socially anarchic, and nearly always RACIST.

**(A) Slice of the cake** Politicians' and trades unionists' way of using five words when they mean one, namely 'share'. No metaphors of sociable food-sharing need be sought: the 'cake' here is derived from the VISUAL AID that makes percentages easy to understand to an increasingly innumerate population, with circles or discs of which various segments (comparable to slices of cake) are shaded or coloured differently to indicate proportions.

**Sloane rangers** A term invented in 1975 (the invention claimed by at least two London wits), a combination of the Lone Ranger (a fictitious film and television character) and Sloane Square or Sloane Street, London, the area where these people are said to range. They are always young and self-consciously fashionable persons of either sex (nearly always aggressively heterosexual and possibly even HETEROSEXIST) and belonging, or aspiring to, the upper, or upper professional, classes. See also YUPPIES.

**Slogan** With so many of the most persistently vocal politicians and agitators coming from Scotland and Ireland it is fitting that this word should be derived from two Gaelic ones, *sluagh* = enemy + *gairm* = a shout. In other words, a war-cry. Today's slogans have unfortunately deteriorated into meaningless repetitions designed to convince the speaker himself that he is communicating with his listeners when in fact he is merely reiterating well-worn formulae. Who can forget Arthur Scargill's famous 'butchering this industry', each of the seven syllables accompanied by one of seven forefinger-waggings?

**Snafu** American forces' slang dating from the Second World War and used by many English people who are not aware of its meaning. Snafu is a sardonic acronymic abbreviation of Situation Normal All Fucked Up. Related subsequent formations include Fubar – Fucked Up Beyond Repair, Fubb – Fucked Up Beyond Belief, Fumtu – Fucked Up More Than Usual; Fubis – Fuck you, Buddy, I'm Shipping Out, which is the American equivalent of the British Army expression, Fuck you, Jack, I'm all right; and Commfu – Complete, monumental military fuck-up.

**Soaps** Media abbreviation of American origin, for soap 'operas'. These started in the later 1940s on American radio (soon also television) – long-running plays released in fifteen-minute instalments that concerned minor domestic dramas, amatory entanglements and medical or other emergencies. Each had a 'cliffhanger' ending to ensure the audience would tune in for the following instalment – and be showered with more advertisements – for each was contrived to mention at least once the name and product of the soap manufacturers sponsoring the programme. (When transferred to television, the soap – later detergent – packet would invariably and contractually be held up to the camera by one of the characters.) All the foregoing, except the sponsorship and the soap packets, now applies to English soaps on both radio and television, including the *Archers* on BBC

Radio, *EastEnders* (thus written – see under INTER-) on BBC
Television, and *Coronation Street* on INDEPENDENT TELEVISION.

**Social(ism)**  A word much misused, and a term of proud
allegiance when applied as a self-description by the LEFT as also
of abuse when said from the RIGHT. It comes from the Latin word
*sociare,* to unite, to have genial or friendly mutual intercourse;
which is highly praiseworthy. But since there are now countless
FACTIONS that all proclaim their own particular brand of socialism
as the only valid one and attack the rest (by gun, bomb or
dialectics), no modern definition is possible. Socialist Realism, in
music and art, under Stalin and most of his successors, meant
music and art so simple that even the stupidest COMMISSAR could
understand it. Hitler also instituted a form of this, though he never
called it National Socialist Realism but, confusingly, Folk Art. The
Social Contract (sometimes also called Social Compact) was the
high-flown name for a wondrously optimistic (and not a little
SIMPLISTIC) proposal in the 1970s by a Labour government to limit
industrial ACTION (i.e. strikes), formulated according to the old-
fashioned Socialist belief that all trades unionists were thoroughly
nice chaps who would abandon such BOLSHY ideas as DIFFERENTIALS
and do as their government told them. The name was borrowed
from Jean-Jacques Rousseau's *Du Contract social* (1762), best
known for its most realistic quotation, *l'homme est né libre, et
partout il est dans les fers* – 'Man is born free and everywhere
he is in chains'. Since the mid-1980s there has arisen another
interesting 'socialist' coinage –

**Social ownership**  Euphemism for CAPITALISM as approved by the
Labour Party. A term coined in the 1986 Party Manifesto. The
Conservatives, who hit on the idea of selling shares, council
houses, etc., to ordinary people, thus making them instant
capitalists, confusingly call it 'People's Capitalism' – in spite of the
fact that the prefix word PEOPLE'S is always a sign of BANANA
Republics and dictatorships.

**Soft left**  One of the many shades of British politics, i.e. not hard
LEFT or MILITANT. The difference is analogous to WETS and dries,
HAWKS AND DOVES, and indeed HARDLINERS AND SOFTLINERS.

**Softly softly** One of the few potentially RACIST expressions that
have not yet been BLACKED or condemned. A COMMUNITY LEADER,
reported in the press, said '.. the Black community favours a softly
softly approach by the racist police to the drugs problem ...' The
man clearly did not know that he was himself being 'racist'. The
full phrase he was alluding to is 'Softly, softly catchee monkey',
meaning that caution (perhaps combined with an element of guile)
is the best way of achieving an end or solving a problem. It is
thought to be of mock-Chinese (see CHINEE) origin, which would
explain why it has not yet been officially banned, for the Chinese
never complain about racial harassment but get on with their work
and – in England – make lovely food and lots of money. However,
the *Cassell Book of Quotations* (p.849, 1970 edition) says it is a
proverb of negro origin.

**Soft-pedal** To state without emphasis, in a LOW KEY – like which it
is based on a misunderstanding of a musical term. The left-hand
(*recte* left-foot) pedal on a piano is colloquially known as the soft
pedal. Although some keyboard instruments of the 18th and early
19th centuries did have pedals that made the sound softer, the
modern 'soft' pedal merely produces a different, slightly thinner,
sound by shifting the keyboard to one side so that fewer strings
are struck with each hammer.

**Soft porn** Sexually EXPLICIT pictures, paintings or ADULT films which
do not show details of genitals, at least not male ones in a
tumescent state, or female ones in close-up.

**Soft target** American euphemism (i.e. a PENTAGONISM) devised in
the Vietnam War to describe the bombing of civilians who were
unable to strike back. TERRORISTS, too, always prefer to attack
women and children rather than armed forces or police. During
the Second World War Winston Churchill spoke of 'the soft
underbelly of Europe', meaning the Italians who (to their credit)
had little stomach for fighting.

**Soft touch** From an American expression for a person who is
known readily to lend or give money. Hence also a term for a
naive person – often even the state, and particularly the WELFARE
STATE – easily defrauded because of the difficulty of checking
claimants' real needs. The current soft touch in Britain is for

anyone who says he lacks a gas or electric cooker to receive a cheque for £150 from the Department of Health and Social Security, without previous or subsequent enquiry. But makers of typewriters may claim a 'soft touch' for their keyboards.

**'Something ought to be done'** King Edward VIII (later Duke of Windsor), on a visit to the depressed areas of South Wales on 18th November 1936, said, 'Something ought to be done to find these people employment,' adding, 'Something will be done.' That 'something' happened three years later, when the Second World War broke out and brought full employment in its wake.

**Sort-of** See IF-YOU-LIKE.

**Soul** A desirable but undefinable quality, especially among black people, some of whom say that whites can never aspire to possessing it – that is, 'soul' without a definite or indefinite article, unlike 'a soul', which is a matter of spirituality, not colour. Prefaced to any word, to make soul-music, soul-sister, etc, it means negro, and indeed the word has its origins in negro jazz, 1940s or earlier. It became a favourite black American word to describe the positive side of negro outlook and culture, reached its height of fashion during the 1970s, and began to wane in the 80s. Soulmates, however, may still be of any colour or ethnic origin. Wentworth & Flexner reveal that in America a soul kiss is 'A long, passionate and open-mouthed kiss, during which a lover's tongue licks, caresses or explores the tongue and mouth of the beloved'.

**(The) .... sound** Music and commercial junk-radio cliché, as in 'the Beatles Sound', 'the Big Band Sound'; and in the naming of pop radio stations, Marcher Sound, etc.

**Spaghetti** Convenient qualifying prefix for things Italian or mock-Italian, e.g. a Spaghetti Western, which is a film of the American wild west type but made – either in Italy or America – with Italian actors and for Italian audiences. (But Spaghetti Junctions are English.) Indian or Chinese equivalents have been described as 'Curry Westerns' or 'Chop Suey Westerns'.

**Spanish athlete** See below.

**Spanish customs** A euphemism for tax- and work-evasion –
especially the kind of dishonest practices traditionally and until
recently engaged in by British newspaper-workers (and
connived at for many years by their employers), e.g. the evasion
of work by demanding and getting payment for a full shift of which
only 45 minutes might be worked; by demanding and getting
overtime pay for no overtime; or merely for HANDLING work that
they were in any case paid to 'handle', i.e. an extra bundle or
two of newspapers. The 'Spanish' element comes from the tax
evasion side of the print-workers' euphemism. Grose's
*Dictionary of the Vulgar Tongue* (1811) says that 'the spanish' was
thieves' slang for ready money, and had been since the end of
the 18th century. And, of course, many of the British print-workers
whose activities are described above worked (again with their
employers' connivance) for cash-in-hand under a variety of
assumed names such as Donald Duck or Clark Gable, so that the
Income Tax authorities would not catch up with them. The
'Spanish' prefix, like Dutch and FRENCH, has many derogatory
applications, since those nations were Britain's traditional
sparring-partners in war. They include 'Spanish Athlete' for one
who talks nonsense or is given to bragging, i.e. a 'bullshitter' (a
word which hardly needs defining); 'Spanish Girdle' or 'Spanish
Padlock' for a chastity-belt; and 'the Spanish Gout', a euphemism
for syphilis. Carpenters would refer to a nail unexpectedly found
in a plank they were sawing as a Spanish Worm.

**Special report** Newspaper euphemism for an artificially-
generated feature article or page, pages, or even a PULL OUT
SUPPLEMENT concerning an industry, a firm, a country or a holiday
resort. The most special thing about Special Reports is that their
main purpose is not to inform readers but to attract lucrative
advertising to the newspaper. Special Reports often also result
in PERKS and FREEBIES for the journalists involved in their
preparation. The *Guardian* is extremely good at selling the
advertising space that warrants the inclusion of a special report,
and is envied by the whole of FLEET STREET for its almost daily
specialist pull-out features. These are called 'Computer Guardian'
or 'Education Guardian' or 'Media File' or 'Society Tomorrow'
and generally consist of one page of articles followed by three of
advertisements – for computer experts, teachers, MEDIA people
or social workers, respectively. One All Fools' Day during the

1970s the *Guardian* published a delightful spoof Special Report extolling the delights of an imaginary country called San Seriffe (the name itself an in-joke for printers and typographers), with advertisements for its holiday paradise, messages of goodwill from its dictator and other ingredients so close to reality that many readers were taken in.

**Spinster** From earliest times this meant a person who spins, and as spinning was nearly always done by women ('Adam delved and Eve span' – the oldest manifestation of SEX-TYPING), spinster became the word for a woman; and from the 17th century, the legal designation of an unmarried one. In the 18th century the word acquired suggestions of one who remained unmarried beyond the usual age for marriage (by which was usually meant child-bearing age), or an old maid. Many women (and not only WIMMIN) not unnaturally object to this, and have successfully campaigned for the abolition of the word from official forms, etc., especially since many a spinster is in fact a COMMON LAW WIFE or SINGLE PARENT with a LOVE CHILD or children.

**Split** The newspapers' invariable description of any political disagreement, however small. See also BANANA.

**Sponsorship** New meanings: 1) a form of advertising by which a firm or other commercial organisation pays for all or part of the expenses incurred in an entertainment venture such as a concert, sports event or a publication, in return for advertising or beneficial publicity. This may range from the crude and pointless exhibition of a product during a television play (by unexpectedly holding it up for viewers to see, as described under SOAP) to a discreet printed acknowledgment in small type. The motives of sponsors vary from the magnanimously altruistic to the self-interestedly incongruous, and are not always to be trusted. Thus a firm making sweets may sponsor research to show that children's teeth derive benefit from being coated in daily doses of sugar, and at least one cigarette manufacturer has sponsored operas at Glyndebourne. The tobacco industry also generously gives much money to medical research – but usually with the strict proviso that such research covers any field but that which might demonstrate the harmful effects of tobacco. Milder forms of sponsorship are accepted by the BBC which, though not

permitted to advertise, prints acknowledgments to concert-
sponsors in its *Radio Times*, yea even to cigarette manufacturers.
2) Charitable activities undertaken with the help of private
sponsors who may contribute an agreed sum of money in
proportion to the object achieved, e.g. sponsored walks at 10p
per mile, sponsored swims, debates, MARATHON concerts, etc.
Although this kind of sponsorship is undertaken for charity those
who attempt to embark on it often do so with mixed motives –
part charitable and part self-publicising or exhibitionistic. See
also –IN.

**Square** Derogatory description by the fashionable of those who
are not; by drug-addicts or pop music FANS of those who are not;
by the generally unkempt and unwashed of those who are thought
to observe VICTORIAN VALUES – although by the time Mrs Margaret
Thatcher had drawn attention to these, the expression had almost
disappeared. Readers may have noticed that this book, in spite
of its traditional shape, is rather square in the views it expresses.

**Squat** An empty or unoccupied house or flat illegally taken over
for their own use by homeless persons, or by persons unable or
unwilling to pay rent. The word was first heard in this sense
during the early 1970s in London. Possession of squats was usually
gained by force, and for some years was held to be 'nine-tenths
of the law', in that the legal owner was unable to regain use of
his home (especially not by using forced entry such as his
uninvited guests had employed). Some confusion was created by
the Greater London Council which in a laudable attempt to ease
the London housing problems declared 'official squats' in
premises it owned but for which it temporarily had no use. Other
'official squats' were available for extremely low rents. The word
was used in Australia as early as 1830, when '... a clan of people
called ''Squatters'' ... generally emancipated convicts ... sat
themselves down in remote situations and maintained large flocks,
obtained generally in very nefarious ways, by having the run of
all the surrounding country' (OED). However, another Australian
source ascribes the origin of squatting to the Americans, whose
'Squatters' Rights' around the middle of the 19th century permitted
them to annex land on which they had settled and which they
then cultivated. Although many English squatters of the 1970s and

80s conscientiously cared for property in which they settled, many others left it in a decidedly unsettled state.

**State of the art** This somewhat highflown description is occasionally given to electrical and other manufactured goods, e.g. radios, television sets and motor-cars. It means the current degree of development of a product, but by implication suggests the highest and most advanced: in other words an ideal cliché for advertisements. Newspapers and even BBC news bulletins have freely been making use of this unusually stilted term without offering further explanation, e.g. 'Police have uncovered a CACHE of state of the art explosives in a wood in Surrey ...' (BBC news!)

**Statutory rape** An offence on the American statute books. The description is increasingly heard in English use, though wrongly applied in this country, where it sounds like a compulsory offence.

**-ster** American suffix of German origin adopted in a few instances into English, like gangster, mobster, teamster, trickster, etc., though it should be pointed out that trickster was ordinary English as early as 1711, and words like SPINSTER go back to older German origins than the Americans ever knew. However, a shyster is not the same as a trickster but an American HOBSON-JOBSON adaptation of the German *Scheiße*=shit. In other words, a shyster might be described as a 'shitster'.

**Stop** As in 'He stopped him in the second round'. Generally a euphemism for knocking out an opponent in the boxing-ring; also used when the victim is so severely damaged that the referee feels obliged to put an end to the licensed brawl that masquerades as a sport. See CONTENDER.

**Stop-out** In English slang, especially in the SCOUSE dialect, a stop-out (perhaps even a 'dirty stop-out') is someone who fails to return home for the evening or night, which he spends in pursuit of some kind of pleasure, usually illicit or unwise. But American stop-outs are students who spend part of their time at university following other pursuits while suspending their studies, in other words those who go MOONLIGHTING. They are therefore temporary DROP-OUTS.

**Storm out** What anyone does when prematurely and suddenly leaving a meeting, perhaps after having disagreed with some of the proceedings or participants. The description is almost unvarying, especially in the media, and is used even if the person steals out silently, slowly and with dignity.

**Strategic redeployment** United States euphemism for a military retreat, or even defeat. This is a PENTAGONESE variation on various old and well-tried formulae, e.g. that used by the British forces during the Second World War, 'Forces of the Eighth Army have taken up previously prepared positions ...'

**(The) Street** Among English journalists this is the customary abbreviation for *Coronation Street,* the long-running SOAP. Only seldom applied to FLEET STREET.

**Street cred** See CRED.

**Street value** There appears to be a naive belief among newsmen and broadcasters that illicit narcotics-dealing never takes place indoors. I would guess that the 'street' prefix is added so as to avoid giving the impression that drugs have a value to respectable people with bank accounts. See also LAUNDERING.

**Streetwise** An Americanism imported into Britain in the early 1970s: said of people (more often children) who are wise, possibly even cunning, about the ways of the streets, their dangers and perhaps also the opportunities found there for committing crime and making money. But see also the -WISE suffix.

**Stringer** A freelance journalist who is employed on a part-time basis to send reports to the MEDIA. Often a mild racket of pseudonymity and MOONLIGHTING, as when a correspondent for one organisation clandestinely feeds news to its rivals. See also LEG MAN.

**Strippagram** See -GRAM.

**Structures** form an important part in modern speech. People who speak of 'restructuring the wages pattern' mean either raising or lowering wages, depending upon whether they are employees

or employers. Many kinds of goods, from bras to typewriters,
are thought to sound a little more desirable to the CONSUMER if
described as structured. And naturally all structures now must
have infrastructures beneath to support them.

**Students** Normally used to describe those undergoing 'further'
education (full- or part-time and usually at a university or
polytechnic), i.e. no longer at primary, secondary, grammar or
comprehensive school. But recent news-usage suggests the need
for additional meanings. Some young persons who are still at
school, in the rush for political CONSENSUS (and egged on by
politically-motivated grown-ups who should know better) feel
they find the old-established description of 'school-children'
demeaning and like to call themselves, rather more grandly,
'school students'. There is even a National Union of School
Students, whose MINI-shop-stewards are presumably even now
demanding to see more pocket money 'on the table right across
the board'. The other kind of 'student' to be treated with suspicion
is any foreigner so described. If he is a visitor to the United
Kingdom, especially from the Middle East, Africa or further afield,
his only qualification for the description might be that he has
enrolled at one of the numerous and sometimes fraudulent
language schools. The real reason for his presence might be
anything from a genuine wish to learn English  and a wish to
qualify for eventual permanent residency, to terrorism, or
merely to his preferring life in this country, with all the benefits
the WELFARE STATE can offer him, as more congenial than life at
home. The third kind of student is also a foreigner, but one who
stays in his own country; and he is not a student at all but a
demonstrator, revolutionary, protester or layabout and mobster,
to whom the euphemistic courtesy-title of 'student' is accorded
by reporters from the BBC and other British news-gathering
bodies. This has now become standard practice, but in following
it the reporters thus invest many hooligans with a status they do
not deserve; although it should be said that in some countries
university lectures are open to all members of the public who
wish to attend, not necessarily those engaged on a full-time
course of studies; and there are therefore in such countries (in
theory at least) more students than would be found elsewhere.
But in most instances, however, when news-reporters say,
'Crowds of students were chanting slogans and throwing missiles

outside the president's palace ...' it may safely be assumed that they have not asked any of the chanters or stone-throwers to produce their student-union card. There may be a certain, carefully calculated, intention of preserving fairness and impartiality (see also FIGHTER) towards foreigners who may rapidly change their status and their clothes – from TERRORISTS' jeans into DIPLOMATS' pinstripes and morning-coats, to be welcomed at the Court of St James's.

**Sunday-** Prefix denoting an amateur activity, or a person who is inexperienced in a particular pursuit or activity because he can follow it only at weekends, e.g. Sunday driver, Sunday carpenter, Sunday cook, etc. But never Sunday astronaut or Sunday brain-surgeon, etc.

**Sunday paper** Usually a euphemism for a Saturday paper, as most Sunday newspapers are on the streets by about 9 pm the night before the nominal date of publication.

**Sunset home** WELFARE STATE euphemism for a place where SENIOR CITIZENS live; in other words, an old people's home; also RESIDENTIAL HOME, although this could equally be a home for younger people who are in some way afflicted or HANDICAPPED. See also TWILIGHT AREA.

**Super-** A very fashionable prefix in the second half of the 20th century. Add it before almost any word and the gullible will consider the result more desirable. Probably first noticed in the *Superman* television and film fantasies. It comes, respectably enough, from the Latin word meaning 'above'.

**Support groups** Heaven knows that in these hard times there are plenty of worthy causes needing and deserving our support, but there are probably now more Support Groups than causes for them to support. Such groups are formed at the slightest opportunity, more for the publicity gained than the support given, their founders secure in the knowledge that they can get full MEDIA publicity at the drop of an ACRONYM. If the events at Gethsemane had happened two thousand years later the Twelve Apostles would doubtless have described themselves as the Jesus Support Group.

**Surreptitious entry** Watergate euphemism (an example of
PENTAGONESE) for burgling or burglary – or, as the Americans
prefer to put it, burglarising or burglarisation.

**Symposium** Strictly, a drinking-party; from the Greek *sumpotes*,
a fellow-drinker. But for the now more customary use see under
SEMINAR.

**Syndrome** A medical term for a combination of two or more
symptoms that may add up to an illness or disorder, from the
Greek meaning 'coming together'. Doctors used to pronounce it
in three syllables, 'syn-droe-may', but then journalists took a
liking to the word and, probably having never heard it but only
seen it written down in learned articles, thought it should have
two syllables. And, as usual, the majority prevails (see PSYCHIATRIC
HOSPITAL). Like 'complex', the word has been appropriated by
cliché users, who happily combine it with any qualifying word to
express almost anything – a habit, a state of affairs, a set of
opinions, a view, etc.

**Synod** The full name is The General Synod of the Church of
England, a governing body set up by that ancient organisation as
recently as 1970, when it was decided to hold a kind of annual
parliament in Church House, London. In this chamber which, like
Parliament, is fitted with doors labelled 'Ayes' and 'Noes' (but has
no LEFT or RIGHT or cross-benchers), clergy as well as laity express
their views and hope to exert influence on the burning issues of
the day – not actually any longer *burning*, but whether women
should be admitted as priests, etc. Unlike the House of Commons
(to date), television cameras are admitted to synod, where they
operate so unobtrusively that the participants soon forget about
them; and then the cameras gleefully zoom in on dozing clerics –
and, on one occasion, on a bishop trying to remove some foreign
substance from his trousers. It has become customary to refer to
this meeting as plain 'synod' without the definite article. Perhaps
the Church feels it already has enough articles; or perhaps it is
because Parliament generally has no article; or because there is
an undue influence of Yorkshiremen, who habitually drop [!]
article from [!] speech. The annual trades union conference, too,
is always referred to as simply 'conference', not 'the conference'.
Synod comes from the Greek word *synodos*, a coming together,

an origin it shares with the Synagogue, the SYNDROME, above, and
the ancient Greek drinking-parties commemorated in the
SYMPOSIUM.

**(The) System** Like the poor, the system is always with us, and
especially for the poor, who have most reason to complain about
it. It means the prevailing political order, the government (of
whatever complexion), the social conditions, the established
class structure (real or imagined), employment (or lack of it).
Even the bosses of a firm may be condemned as being 'part of
the system'. Whatever this system is held to be, the complainer
does not belong to it and disapproves of it. And even if he
becomes a millionaire he is likely to complain about the system
which by taxing his wealth deprives him of a large part of it. Tax
evasion is his way of beating the system, while the poor beat the
system by joining the BLACK economy. 'System' in this anarchic
political sense dates back to the early years of the 19th century
and has been in French and German use even longer.

# T

**Tabloids** Newspapers approximately half the size of BROADSHEETS.
The latter are traditional in this country (the oldest free press),
and by their impressive size suggest probity and authority. A
tabloid newspaper (not really a *news*paper but an entertainment
sheet) generally contains about a tenth of the news and features
found in a large paper, which may cost only a few coppers more.
The origin of the word 'tabloid' is to be found in the copyright
trade-name of an English patent-medicine, the property of
Burroughs, Wellcome and Company Ltd. (now the Wellcome
Foundation). In about 1880 the chemist Sir Henry Wellcome
invented a method of making small, highly-compressed medicinal
tablets which could be easily taken by mouth, for, until then,
patients had to take their medicines either by powder or as big
tablets ('horse-pills'). He combined the Greek -*oid* ending with
part of 'tablet', and his tabloid was an instant success. So much so
that the word became a common synonym of anything small –
used exactly like the word MINI in the 20th century. So when Sir
Thomas Sopwith made a small fighter-plane at the beginning of

the First World War he called it the Sopwith Tabloid. Tabloid
newspapers did not arrive until about 1925, when the Fleet Street
magnate Lord Northcliffe proposed the establishment of what he
described informally in a speech as 'a tabloid newspaper' – much
as someone might now say 'a mini newspaper'. Most tabloids are
sensational in content, slapdash in style, and noted for their
frequent disregard of grammar and spelling; and their writers
claim to be on first-name terms with everyone, however old
and/or distinguished ('Neil Slams Maggie'). They seldom correct
their inaccuracies (or, if forced by legal action to do so, do it in
the most inconspicuous way possible); and they constantly repeat,
in the same pseudo-jocular or stilted language, non-news under
headlines that make up in size for what they lack in clarity or
sense.

**Tactical air support** Pentagonese euphemism for bombing.

**Taffia** In facetious use, i.e. without any suggestions of criminality,
a reference to the existence of an alleged Welsh MAFIA.

**Tailback** An Americanism which, like 'commuter', has usefully
and happily settled down in British English. It means a traffic
queue or blockage. Tie-up and snarl-up are less often heard in
the UK.

**Take out** Euphemism for a murder or assassination. A gangster's
moll should treat with suspicion her boyfriend's proposal to 'take
her out'.

**Talking head** A generally derisive description of a television-
presenter, usually one who reads a script in a programme which
has no illustrations, photographs, films or other VISUAL AIDS – one
which is in fact just like a radio programme except that the
presenter is seen as well as heard. The irony is that the words he
reads are usually not his own but those written by a GHOST, script-
writers or RESEARCHERS.

**Tawdry** see MAUDLIN.

**Technology park** New euphemism for the old Industrial Estate.
See PARK.

**Television personalities** People who are famous for being
famous, which invariably means because they are often seen on
television. They may be very slightly accomplished in some other
field, e.g. as cartoonists, pop entertainers or starlets, or merely
well known for having big breasts (in one case, for having
exposed them at a rugby match). But personalities become
personalities mostly BECAUSE (THEY ARE) THERE, initially perhaps
employed to read the television news or otherwise speak words
that are not their own, often quiz questions set by others (see
RESEARCHERS). Thereafter a television personality can command
huge sums for opening bazaars, the ENDORSEMENT of commercial
products or having books written under his name by GHOST
writers and PACKAGED on his behalf and then published as if he
were a real author. And of course he can be seen most afternoons
on television chat shows or panel games. This process continues
in ever smaller, incestuously spiralling, circles until someone
(never the public, which has no say in the personalities' creation
in the first place) decides that he or she has been exposed enough
and should be dropped. After that, personalities often find that as
excessive and exaggerated success wanes, one door closes and
another slams in their face; and they may end up leading lonely
lives, taking to drink, shoplifting or becoming NAMES at Lloyd's.
Pop personalities usually wear SHADES even when the sun is not
shining.

**Tell that to the marines** A saying which, according to
Partridge's *Dictionary of Slang and Unconventional English*
(Routledge), dates from the early 19th century. Less elegantly
expressed by Americans as 'Oh yeah?', it means 'I don't believe
it'. Marines were sea-going soldiers, who were barely tolerated
by real sailors, or even despised by them for their proneness to
seasickness, their innocence of the lore of the sea, in short, their
general unseaworthiness. Thus they found themselves the butt of
practical jokes, credulous of every tall story the sailors cared to
tell them. Hence the phrase, meaning, 'the marines may believe
you, but you can't fool a real sailor'. During the Second World
War a family received a censored post-card from their son, a
prisoner-of-war in Germany, which read, 'We have plenty of food
and are being treated well. Please tell this to Alastair and Arthur.'
His brothers Alastair and Arthur were in the Royal Marines, so

the family knew what he was trying to say. See also YOMPING, a
word the Royal Marines claimed to have invented.

**-teria** American suffix denoting a serve-yourself establishment,
from *cafeteria* (which is in fact a Spanish word for a coffee-pot
and was the original coffee-shop so named – just as its English
equivalent might be named 'The Singing Kettle'). According to the
*Dictionary of American English* Chicago had a Cafetiria in 1894,
and several others by 1895, with a spelling change to Cafetéria
a year later. American catering and commerce invented self-
service, and so the suffix -eria in due course came to denote this;
and in recent decades has suffered adaptations and modifications,
e.g. fruiteria, lunchateria, grocerteria, washateria, etc. See also
-ORIUM and -RAMA.

**Termination with extreme prejudice** Assassination, said to be
a CIA jargon-euphemism. See also TAKING OUT. In medical talk,
'termination' appears to be the normal euphemistic abbreviation
of 'termination of pregnancy', i.e. abortion.

**Terrorist** See FREEDOM FIGHTER.

**Test drive** From the jargon of motor-car advertisements, now
applied, often facetiously, to any other consumer product, even to
foodstuffs ('Test drive one of our sausages . . .').

**That I must see** American-Jewish inversion. It is a literal, word-
for-word translation of the common German phrase, *Das muss
ich sehen.* Infinitely variable, e.g. 'That I must try . . .' etc.

**Thatcherism** Mrs Margaret Thatcher, Member of Parliament and
the first woman Prime Minister in this country, is the only head of
a British government whose policies have given rise to an *ism*
based on her name, though the word is chiefly used as a term of
abuse or derogation. See BUTSKELLISM for the nearest other British
politicians came to this accolade.

**Theatre of . . .** Critics' jargon. The Theatre of Cruelty/The Theatre
of the Absurd/ . . . of Participation/ . . . of Realism, etc.

**Theme park** American name, now increasingly common in
Britain, for an amusement park or area devoted to a certain

unifying theme or subject that obtains there. The replica 18th-century American town of Williamsburg, Virginia, is an early example, though it has never been given this description. See also PARK.

**'There's no call for it'** Shopkeepers' euphemism for 'We can't be bothered to stock it'.

**Thermal underwear** Warm underwear, to which commerce tries to lend extra desirability by using the Greek-based word for warmth.

**(The) thinking ...** Advertising jargon by which machines (usually those containing elements of computerisation, or even quite ordinary features of automation) are made to appear to have been invested with the power of thought, e.g. 'The Thinking Dishwasher', or 'The Thinking Coffee Grinder'.

**The thinking man's ...** The original object of this now common saying is thought to have been 'the thinking man's crumpet', applied to Joan Bakewell, a television journalist both intelligent and comely. Many variations are heard.

**(The) third world** Although the First and Second Worlds are seldom described  by their numbers, the First World, by customary implication, is the Western Alliance, i.e. Nato, especially Great Britain and America; and the Second consists of the USSR and the communist bloc. The Third, which is the most talked and written about, consists of supposedly unaligned nations which have allegiance to neither the East nor the West, but accept financial aid from both superpower blocs – who lend or donate it (see RESCHEDULED DEBTS) with a keen eye on what they can get in return – usually either military bases or strategic exports. Such aid is looked upon by some former British dependencies as a moral debt (and they may have a case), but this does not prevent them from heaping abuse and accusations of RACISM on the former mother-country when it suits them. The concept of three worlds was first propounded by politicians in the mid-1950s. It should be added that according to some interpretations the Chinese hold the view that they, not the Russians and their satellites, constitute the Second World.

Another thing that distinguishes the Third World from the other two is its large numbers of proletarians; and also that it has taken its revenge on the First by growing, and supping it with, apparently limitless supplies of narcotics.

**This has restored my faith in British justice**  Comment often heard from successful defendants or litigants in British courts of law. Those who lose their case may resort to 'The law is an ass'. See also SHOW TRIAL.

**-thon**  See MARATHON.

**Thriller**  H.L. Mencken says this is the American word for what the English used to call a 'shocker', i.e. 'a work of fiction of a sensational character' (OED). But the English word has long given way in England to the American one. Try asking in a bookshop for 'a paperback shocker'.

**Thrilling**  Today this is applied to something that is full of pleasurable excitement, like a THRILLER, above. But it is a comparatively new meaning. A paragraph in the *Musical Times* of May 1912 reporting the heroic demeanour of the band of the *Titantic* begins, 'The story of the foundering of the *Titanic* early on Monday morning, April 15, has thrilled civilised humanity.'

**Through (thru)**  American for 'until', as in 'Monday thru Friday'. It is also used to mean 'up to and including', as in a book entitled *Chamber Music Brahms through Stravinsky*.

**Timeline**  This is what we now have to call what used to be the Speaking Clock, or usually, TIM – because those were the letters one dialled when there were still alphabetical as well as numeric ways of DIALLING – and indeed when there were still dials. The Post Office telephone system has become British Telecom, and Telecom has hired out its speaking clock, or 'Timeline', to a company selling watches.

**Time out**  The new, American-based, way of saying 'time off'. Even in Parliament MPs are heard to say, during Question Time, 'Will the Prime Minister take time out . . .?'

**Toilet** Euphemism, and an inaccurate one at that, for a LAVATORY.

**Toke** Advertising, media and stage slang for a 'token' member of a minority group. According to the unwritten 'toke' rule, any group of children shown in a television advertisement must include one black and one Asian child. And where SEX-TYPING is not part of the action (e.g. when the commercial does not depict, perhaps, a group of young male hooligans noisily swilling beer in a drinks commercial) women's minority RIGHTS workers are likely to be up in arms if a token woman is not included. Chinese and Jews are less sensitive about being left out of such groupings. See also EQUAL OPPORTUNITIES.

**Total recall** Cliché for a good memory, or, in the case of politicians who claim to have it, recalling what they wish to reveal.

**Train captain** Grand new name for the railway guard on the New London Docklands Railway. This improvement in rank was doubtless due to the fact that these trains are driverless, an innovation which is sure to lead to demands for increased wages from the guards; and the award of an impressive title always pleases a recipient.

**Trash** American for what an Englishman calls rubbish; and his rubbish-bin is the American trash-can. The word is thought to be related to various Norse, Swedish, Icelandic and Norwegian words like *trask, tros, trasa*, etc, meaning such discarded objects as fallen timber fragments, rotten leaves, rags and tatters. A Bill in Chancery of 1555 laid down a ruling about 'A carpenter's yarde wherein he dothe laye his tymber and trasshe . . .'

**Tree surgeon** One of the many professional euphemisms by which those who follow certain honourable trades attempt to make their calling sound grander. A man who prunes trees (or even fells them, when he might be called a 'tree killer') may, of course, be a qualified arboriculturalist – 'one who cultivates trees or shrubs for use or ornament' (OED), which is surely as grand a job-title as anyone could wish for. But many mere tree-fellers prefer to echo the Second Commoner in Shakespeare's *Julius Caesar* who says proudly, 'Truly, sir, all I live by is the awl . . . I am, indeed, sir, a surgeon to old shoes.'

**Trick or treat** 'The custom of going from house to house on Halloween asking for small gifts and playing tricks on people who refuse to give,' says the *Dictionary of American Idioms*, Boatner/Gates/Makkai (1975). This ancient and harmless American children's folk-custom has been imported into Britain and adapted as a Guy Fawkes' Day activity which sometimes turns into a minor extortion racket. And, just as children start asking for the now anachronistic 'Penny for the Guy' by the end of summer, so is tricking-or-treating almost an all-year-round activity.

**Truck** American for a lorry, a word which is gaining ground in Britain. Their truck farmer is what we call a market gardener; and an American haulier's firm is a truck line.

**Trunk** American for what Englishmen call the boot of their car. The Englishman's bonnet is an American's hood, both originally items of clothing.

**Tug-of-love child** Media jargon for a child whose custody is disputed by parents, either husband disputing with wife or, more rarely, adoptive against real parents. The allusion is to the game of tug-of-war, and the Judgment of Solomon irony of tearing the child limb-from-limb apparently escapes the media parrots who use the term as a kind of shorthand. See also LOVE CHILD.

**Turbo** From the Latin for a whirlwind. When the manufacturer of an apparatus with revolving parts, such as a motor-car, vacuum-cleaner or electric food-mixer brings out a more expensive model it is almost axiomatic that it will bear the additional word turbo so as to impress the customer. In mechanics and engineering, however, the turbine, and hence the turbo- prefix, have a respectable ancestry.

**Turf accountant** Euphemism for a bookmaker.

**Tut** An Englishman's expression of mild disapproval, often reduplicated as tut-tut. But when Americans speak of a tut they mean a paper-bag – a HOBSON-JOBSON approximation of the German *Tüte*. In Scotland a paper-bag, or tut, is called a poke (hence the expression 'a pig in a poke' for something bought unseen). It is therefore perfectly in order to ask a Scottish shop-assistant, 'Can I have a poke?'

**Twilight areas** A term said to have been invented by Richard Crossman in his *Diaries* (ed. Janet Morgan, Hamish Hamilton, 1975) for INNER CITY areas allegedly ready for demolition: 'A Labour minister should impose central leadership, large-scale state intervention, in these blighted areas of cities, the twilight areas, which were once genteelly respectable but are now rotting away'; but Sir Keith Joseph also used the expression in 1960. It soon became a planners' euphemism, and whenever they used it people knew that their distinctive old houses would soon be demolished and replaced by concrete towers and boxes. But in the event it was the Conservatives who realised that twilight heralded not only impending darkness but also the dawn. Michael Heseltine, as Minister for the Environment, and John Patten, as a Housing Minister, during the 1980s, instigated great schemes for urban preservation, restoration and renovation of ancient domestic buildings.

**Twinning** Of British towns and cities: the establishment of a 'special relationship' claimed to exist between places in different countries. The declared aim is one of international friendship, but in practice all it means is that councillors and local-government officials get free holiday trips at their rate-payers' expense. LOONY LEFT councils are often recognised by the totalitarian company they keep when getting themselves twinned; and one such council, in its eagerness to spend its rate-payers' money, even employs an official with the grandiose title 'Municipal Twinning Co-ordinator'. See also FREEBIE.

**Tycoon** An important businessman. The word is an American adoption from the Japanese word *taikun*, great lord or prince (itself from the Chinese *ta*= great + *kiun*= prince) a title by which the hereditary commander-in-chief of the JAP army was described to foreigners by the Japanese people. The first American (or indeed Westerner) to be described as a tycoon is thought to have been President Lincoln, in 1861.

**Typo** This, you would think, must be an abbreviation of 'typographer' (see the -o abbreviation and suffix) but it is in fact a euphemistic term common among newspapermen when they speak of a typographical error. Perhaps they are ashamed to use the words in full because they make so many of these errors.

# U

**Ugandan discussions** Euphemism for sexual intercourse, a term coined by the satirical magazine *Private Eye* after it carried a report about a couple, one a prominent Ugandan diplomat, caught in a compromising situation. They unconvincingly explained that all they were doing was 'discussing Ugandan affairs'.

**Umbrella** From the Latin word *umbra* = shade, and an Italian invention; but the device is in less sunny climates more often used as a protection against the rain. Coryat's *Crudities* in 1611 reported that some people in Italy carried '. . . fine things which they commonly call in the Italian tongue "umbrellaes". These are made of leather something answerable to the forme of a little canopy and hooped on the inside with divers little wooden hoopes that extend the umbrella in a pretty large compass.' In the 20th century umbrellas have been put to figurative uses, e.g. the wartime 'umbrella fighter cover', which was supposed to keep enemy bombers away, and, latterly, 'umbrella organisations' or 'umbrella bodies', which are fashionable names for groups comprised of separate bodies having like interests – perhaps to afford protection to GRASS ROOTS.

**Unacceptable** One of the most over-used vogue words in the WELFARE STATE among people who are quite properly and understandably anxious to obtain their 'rights', often with the help of RIGHTS MOVEMENTS. Its introduction relates to a statement by the then Prime Minister, Edward Heath, made on 15th May 1973 in reply to a parliamentary question. It captured the imagination of all LEFT-wingers to such an extent that 'unacceptable' has become so cherished a word among the dissatisfied and disaffected (and not only among LOONIES), and has been well and truly flogged to death. There is, however, some misunderstanding about the exact origin of the statement. *The Times* attributed it direct to the Prime Minister at his press conference at Conservative Central

Office on 16 June 1970. However, it was later established that it
was merely in the text of the press release (No. G.E.228) handed
out at the conference. And the words of press releases, like those
of prepared speeches, cannot always be attributed to politicians
but may be the work of speech-writers or officials (see GHOST). But
according to Hansard, the record of parliamentary proceedings,
Mr Heath did say, in the House of Commons on 15th May 1973, 'It
is the unpleasant and unacceptable face of capitalism, but one
should not suggest that the whole of British industry consists of
practices of this kind.'

**Uncle Tomism** The eponymous hero of Harriet Beecher Stowe's
anti-slavery novel *Uncle Tom's Cabin* is now thought by some
militant blacks to have been too friendly and/or respectful to
whites. Hence 'Uncle Tomist' for any black man considered to be
working with instead of against (THE) SYSTEM. See also OREO, AFRO-
SAXON.

**Under-achievers** All too often this refers to dull or lazy children
who do badly at school, often through no fault of their own, but
who must be protected by educationalists' euphemisms at
establishments where scholastic competition is disapproved of
by progressives.

**Underdeveloped** See EMERGENT.

**Underlying** One of the many modern filler-words that add
nothing except bulk (and possibly rhythm) to a sentence, as in 'the
underlying cause for the outbreak . . .' However, there are many
valid applications for the word, as when something 'underlies'
in the sense of a hidden undercurrent or a reason not immediately
apparent. The suffix -ATION also lends superfluous bulk to many
words.

**Underprivileged** Another euphemism for the poor or
DISADVANTAGED.

**Unisex** Slang word dating from the late 1960s denoting something
that is considered suitable for, or can be used by, both men and
women, e.g. a hairstyle, articles of clothing, lavatories, etc. – and,
more recently, language that is free from SEX-TYPING and cleansed

of all sexist implications. See CHAIR, WIMMIN and the various cross-references they point to.

**Unknown quantity** When someone says of another person, 'He's an unknown quantity' he really means '. . . of unknown *quality*'.

**Untitled** Oxymoronic title favoured by modern painters to name their unnamed pictures, e.g. 'Untitled 1987' or 'Untitled XII' – though with never a hint of jest or irony. There is no reason why artists *should* give names to their pictures, but describing paintings as 'Untitled' (even when they are traditionally representational and might be called 'Mother and Child', or 'Landscape with Bananas', etc.) has become a trendy, faddy thing to do, just like CONTEMPORARY composers' predilection for snappy, meaningless (or obscurely Greek) one-word titles followed by Roman numerals, e.g. 'Nexus IV'.

**Unwarranted intrusion** Few intrusions are warranted. The extra word adds force rather than meaning.

**Unwinding** Euphemistic exuse for having a holiday. Also RECHARGING BATTERIES.

**U-turn** A change of direction which is seldom permitted on the roads and never admitted in politics, where, when it happens, it is described as pragmatism.

**Unwaged** 'Unwaged admitted half-price'. People not drawing a wage or salary. A new euphemism for 'unemployed'. The uneasy implication is that to pay someone is to 'wage' him. See also BETWEEN JOBS, CLAIMANTS, REDUNDANT, CONSULTANCY.

# V

**Vatican roulette** An adaptation of RUSSIAN ROULETTE and applied to the 'rhythm' method of contraception which relies on the supposedly safe period. For obvious reasons it is also known as the 'rhythm-and-blues' method (see BLUE in the Colour Supplement). And while on the subject, see also CONDOM.

**Vending** Selling has acquired many different forms, including 'marketing' and 'merchandising'; but vending means selling from a coin-operated slot-machine.

**Victorian values** A term used by Mrs Margaret Thatcher during the early 1980s in several speeches and utterances in which she advocated a return to the moral standards of a bygone age but failed to mention the poverty and deprivation many Victorians suffered. And almost as soon as she said it, an INSIDER DEALING scandal revealed that the CITY's idea of Victorian values was rather different from hers.

**Vigilantes** In the lawless South America of about 1860, these were committees of private citizens banded together to keep order and enforce some kind of policing. The resulting justice was often rough, but lawbreakers were discouraged, at least until official police forces were organised. Hence this Spanish word, which originally meant a nightwatchman, privately employed to guard property, like the *askari* in Africa. Vigilantes are being revived in modern Britain by residents who feel the police is not protecting them enough (while at the same time law-breakers complain of OVER-POLICING!) Such groups are within the law only if they do not attempt to punish those they catch. These arrangements are now usually called NEIGHBOURHOOD WATCH schemes.

**Village** As English villages are disappearing, losing their village schools and village charm, many of them (at least those within COMMUTING range of London) turn into weekend retreats for the rich. And as these villages decline, brand-new ones with brand-new houses are springing up everywhere, even in the former INNER CITIES. These are generally speculative city (or CITY) developments whose only quaintness lies in their name. (See also PARK.) Another kind of village is the alleged GLOBAL village, a romantic idea based on the absurd premise that all men are not only brothers but also good neighbours, who far from wanting to kill each other will wish to borrow the traditional half-cup of sugar from each other. Even more incongruous is the modern misuse of HAMLET – formerly more rural than the village (i.e. one so small that it has neither church nor parish-council) but now a favoured word for newly-created TWILIGHT AREAS with architect-

designed urban decay and deprivation, e.g. Tower Hamlets in
London.

**-ville** Sardonic American suffix denoting and describing the
alleged quality or nature of a place, e.g. Dullsville, Dragsville,
Drugsville, etc. Presumably derived from American place-names
of French origin. See also ALLEY.

**Violation** American for an offence under the law. An
Englishman's traffic offence is an American's traffic violation. The
American form is, however, now becoming so common in Great
Britain that it has (in that particular sense) acquired the status of
a fashionable neologism.

**Visual aid** Neologism meaning a picture, diagram or drawing,
made in order to illustrate facts, trends, opinions, etc., for example,
by illustrating a percentage figure as a SLICE OF THE CAKE, or a firm's
sales figures with graphs – see BOTTOMING OUT.

**Vital statistics** As a term this has been in common use since at
least 1837, when a book entitled *Vital Statistics; or the Statistics of
Health, Sickness, Diseases and Death* was published. But the
advent of GIRLIE magazines in the 1950s and, a littler later, the
publication of naked or semi-naked women in vulgar TABLOID
newspapers, almost monopolised the term to mean the breast,
waist and hip measurements of women. So much so that the
original, correct, meaning would now be misunderstood and
probably cause merriment.

**Vow** Noun and verb: a JOURNOS' hyperbole term meaning a
perfectly ordinary, mundane decision, or to make such a
decision, e.g. 'He vowed to go to the shops and buy a packet of
cigarettes.'

# W

**Wages differential** See ELITISM.

**(Going) walkies** Dog-owners' euphemism for fouling
pavements, roads, parks, woods and fields with excrement, i.e.

dogs 'doing their business', or leaving the animals' CALLING-CARD. 'Walkies' is based on the pretence that the animal takes its owner for a walk, not the other way, suggesting that the animal controls its own actions. But the ultimate responsibility for disgusting urban pavements still rests with the owner, not the dog.

**Wall to wall** An expression denoting, at first, comprehensiveness, completeness, and (in its original application to carpets) luxuriousness; but also now, figuratively, an excess, e.g. wall-to-wall symphonies, wall-to-wall chambermaids, wall-to-wall MUZAK, etc. In the British armed forces, some civil-service departments and the diplomatic service, the higher ranks get wall-to-wall carpets in their office and/or their official residences. Lower ranks may also get carpets, but the uncovered parts nearer the walls are in proportionate size to rank or grade. The lower the rank the smaller the carpet. In the BBC for many years only the corridors ('of power'?) in Broadcasting House that lead to the Director-General's office on the third floor were covered with carpets. The rest had linoleum.

**Wally** See WIMP.

**Walter Plinge** Theatrical euphemism for a person, or imaginary person. In sport and other activities a participant whose identity is not known at the time of printing, or one who does not exist at all, may also be described as A. N. Other. In theatrical cast-lists Walter Plinge may disguise the fact that one actor is doubling on several parts, or the fact that a distinguished actor who, for one reason or another (usually lack of work), is obliged to accept a role he considers beneath him, wishes to save his reputation by remaining anonymous. In the programmes of Glyndebourne Festival Opera Walter Plinge has a way of appearing (together with his slightly less famous brother Gerald) in suitably international disguises, e.g. Waltraut von Plingenheim, Valéry Plinge etc. Plinge's American counterpart is George Spelvin; and in the SOFT-PORN American film *Indecent Exposure*, shown occasionally on British television, one of the characters appears in the cast-list as Georgina Spelvin – the real actress probably wishing to remain anonymous. In some of the plays by Henry Livings there is a non-existent character called James (Jimmy) Dickinson who always fails to appear on stage. See also JOHN DOE.

**Warts and all** Common misquotation of a phrase attributed to Oliver Cromwell and found in Horace Walpole's *Anecdotes of Painting*: 'Mr Lely, I desire you would use all your skill to paint my picture truly like me, and not flatter me at all; but remark these roughnesses, pimples, warts, and everything as you see me, otherwise I will never pay a farthing for it.'

**Washing hands** Old English euphemism for emptying one's bladder. When a hostess says 'Would you like to wash your hands?' do not say, 'Thanks, I'll use the kitchen sink.'

**Wasp** American acronymic abbreviation of White Anglo-Saxon Protestant. See also the less common AFRO-SAXON; also OREO. Christopher Hitchens has suggested (in the *Times Literary Supplement*, 14 November 1986) that the redundant W should be eliminated from the term. He asked if there were any BASPS and added, 'doesn't ASP convey precisely the same connotation with even more economy?'

**Waste recycling receptacle** Local government euphemism for a rubbish bin. A 'Household Waste Amenity Point' has also been seen.

**-Watch** Vogue suffix, especially for titles of television and other programmes, e.g. *Foxwatch, Childwatch, Petwatch, Crimewatch, Drugwatch, Aidswatch, Roadwatch, Neighbourhood Watch*. Sometimes also-Watchers, e.g. Weight-watchers, etc. See also VIGILANTES, SEX TYPING and below.

**Watchdogs** In *The Tempest*, Shakespeare's 'watch-dogges barke bowgh wawgh', but these are real canine ones. Today the word is almost exclusively used for committees and other organisations meant to protect the citizen against injustices or other wrong-doings by the state or officialdom. Such 'watchdog bodies' come in two breeds – with or without teeth.

**We are providing a service** Self-justificatory catch-phrase used by persons (often during the course of interviews) whose activities may be disreputable and widely disapproved of but legal, e.g. making purses from kittens, dog-meat from horses or participating in the various forms of prostitution. Hitler's lampshade-makers doubtless had a German expression for it.

**Weenies** A HOBSON-JOBSON corruption-modification-diminution of 'Wiener', i.e. *Wiener Würstel*, Viennese sausages, invented by the American fast-food industry and which have little to do with sausages and even less with Vienna.

**Welfare state** A term often attributed to the economist and former Liberal MP, Lord Beveridge (1879–1963), or else to Sir Alfred Zimmern (1879–1957), although the earliest appearance in print known to the OED occurs in a book by Archbishop William Temple (1881–1944), who wrote in 1941, 'We have seen ... that in place of the conception of the Power-State we are led to that of the Welfare-State.' After the Second World War Beveridge was commissioned by Attlee's idealist Labour government to formulate its principles and it was duly inaugurated – minus the hyphen which the meticulous Archbishop insisted upon. Much has happened since the introduction of the Welfare State, and some say it has turned into a NANNY STATE which saps initiative and kills enterprise. But whatever the shortcomings and however its critics denigrate it, the British Welfare State is still the envy of the rest of the world.

**Wets** Left-wing English Conservative politicians who take a softer, more conciliatory attitude to the trades unions and are not entirely against the WELFARE STATE (although the concept of 'left' and 'right' is in this context itself a subdivision of a grouping that is already to the right of the old-fashioned LEFT). More right-wing conservatives are, by a rather clumsy analogy, called 'drys' (sometimes 'dries'). The American counterparts are HAWKS AND DOVES (or HARDLINERS AND SOFTLINERS) though these in turn reflect views more related to international than national affairs. There were wets and drys (or dries) in the United States also during the prohibition period – but at that time it was the wets who were the more progressive, as they advocated a reform of the draconian anti-alcohol laws, whereas the drys, like the MAFIA, wanted prohibition to continue. People who were formerly described as being wet in a non-political way, e.g. CHINLESS WONDERS, are now more likely to be either wallies or WIMPS.

**Whistle-blowing** The practice of informing on one's colleagues and superiors, as for example, by publishing details of commercial or government malpractice, incompetence or excessive profit-making; or material otherwise embarrassing to the rich, famous, powerful or influential. The original whistle-blower was the American CONSUMERIST Ralph Nader, who single-handedly exposed dangerous American motor-cars and caused wide-ranging changes to be made. See also INVESTIGATIVE JOURNALISM.

**Whitehat** See HARDHAT.

**Whitewash** 'Such as are blackened in the *North Briton* . . . are white-washed in the *Auditor* . . .' wrote a JOURNALIST in 1762. Whitewashing (derived from 'the painting over of blemishes on walls, etc') in this sense means to give the appearance of innocence or to free someone from blame, or fault, or to cover up and conceal guilt. The word is thus used only by those who hold that the cover-up was mistaken, e.g. when a person they consider guilty is pronounced innocent before the law; never by the person acquitted or exonerated. In the United States, a 'white-washed American' is a person (of any colour) who, although not a WASP, tries hard to emulate one – see also OREO. It is a curious fact that every time a white person is acquitted in an English court of having harmed a black, other blacks complain vociferously and explicitly of 'whitewash' – without apparently noticing any verbal incongruity. This is borne out by numerous newspaper reports.

**Whole** Coming from the same root as *heal*, *hale* and *hail*, whole was a natural candidate for adoption by ecologists, environmentalists and health-food addicts to describe anything wholesome, entire, healthy and (supposedly) pure. The term Whole Food has become an almost inseparable pair of BUZZ WORDS, with the additional element of ORGANIC. But you can't have everything; and food which has *not* been subjected to the many and various artificial (and quite possibly harmful) purification processes by the food industry may well be more likely to contain natural and unwholesome creatures like beetles and weevils (free-range, no doubt). Proponents of healthy eating have also taken a fancy to the words 'wholism' and 'wholistic', which were coined by philosophers in the 1930s and have nothing to do with health. To be a 'whole man' is a desirable state of being and is now usually taken to mean a virile one in full working possession of his sex organs. In fact it originally related to the earlier meanings given above, as in St Matthew IX, 12 'They that are whole need not a physician, but that they are sick.' For another curious health-food-fad usage see MACROBIOTICS.

**Whose ... is it anyway?** Headline and title cliché steming from a play entitled *Whose Life is it Anyway?* by Brian Clark.

**Willie** (Now more rarely Willy) *English Dialect Dictionary* (1905): 'An infantile name for the penis'. Peter Fryer, in *Mrs Grundy: Studies in English Prudery* (Corgi, 1963), says it dates from 'before 1847' and also gives the (formerly more common) John Thomas; as well as Jack, Jack Robinson, Jack-in-the-box, Jock, Dick (and Dickie), Captain Standish, Sir Martin Wagstaff – all the way up the social scale to The Bishop or His Majesty (both 'in Purple Cap').

**Wimmin** A facetious phonetic mis-spelling of 'women' used by many writers (including H. G. Wells), at first in order to characterise a certain speech accent. But in the late 1970s it began to be used as a conscious mis-spelling favoured by feminists anxious to eliminate the -man or -men elements from their vocabulary. See also the manifestations of UNISEX English exemplified by CHAIR. See also PERSON.

**Wimp** Vogue word for a supposedly feeble, weak or ineffectual person, a kind of non-political WET, or a wally. Although this has come into fashionable use only recently (especially by YUPPIES, who consider themselves the very opposite of wimps), the original expression (according to specialised dictionaries) denoted a whining dog, and, by extension, a man who is constantly complaining about something. Wallies are like wimps but more stupid, and not necessarily weak.

**Wireless** The earlier name of what is now called radio, but often revived for facetious purposes. Even more facetious is 'steam radio', a term intended to make radio sound even more old-fashioned – by suggesting, falsely, that up-to-date people only watch television. In reality there is an increasing number of viewers deserting that often repetitious, puerile and trivialising

medium and returning to radio fare as offered by BBC Radio
Three and Radio Four.

**-Wise** American suffix meaning 'in the manner of', popularised
by German-speaking immigrants to the United States of America.
In their language the -*weise* suffix is far more common than in
English and is used to make all manner of words or to express
certain concepts. Hence expressions like 'Holidaywise I feel
deprived', or 'What would you like ice-creamwise?' But see also
STREETWISE, in which the last element of the word denotes wisdom.

**Within the framework of...** Clumsy Americanism which is a
literal translation from the German *Im Rahmen des/der*... Usually
better expressed by 'In the context of ...' or simply 'As ...'

**Workerist** One of the POSITIVE *isms* of the LEFT meaning someone
who is sympathetic to the working man and the proletarian class-
struggle; often a WHITE-collar worker who espouses the cause of
working-class people – and is perhaps duly despised by them
for his paternalistic attitude.

**Workshop** Not now necessarily a place where manual or
mechanical work is done but, in the arts, when preceded by
other words such as 'Theatre', 'Music', 'Poetry', etc, a place where
some kind of entertainment takes place, possibly in a self-
consciously daring or experimental manner. The suffix was first
used in the United States in the 1930s but took several decades to
spread to Britain.

**World** The presence of this word in titles generally implies a
size, scope or comprehensiveness not always borne out by reality.
Thus a gramophone record containing three or four pieces of
music by Vivaldi might be entitled 'The World of Vivaldi'.
Preceded by a possessive case – *Whicker's World, Gardeners'
World*, etc. – it lends weight to television programmes or book
titles. The American fairground *Disney World* may not have
started the trend but certainly helped to perpetuate it, and has
led to many THEME PARKS in Britain with 'world' titles. In 1986 all
Butlins Holiday Camps were renamed *Butlins Holiday World*.

**(The) world is (his) oyster** A common misquotation from
Shakespeare's *The Merry Wives of Windsor* ('Why, then the
world's mine oyster, which I with sword will open....') The phrase
is intended to suggest unlimited possibilities for the fortunate
possessor of this particular mollusc. 'The world was Karajan's
oyster. Suddenly the question was: could little Jimmy Galway get
in there and be a pearl in that oyster?' (James Galway, in *An
Autobiography*, writing about his successful audition to join the
Berlin Philharmonic Orchestra.)

**Would you buy a used car from this man?** A pertinent question
asked about Richard M. Nixon (and, as it turned out in the light
of subsequent events, a prescient one) when he was running
against John F. Kennedy in the American Presidential elections
of 1960. Since then it has been a standard American test of
someone's probity and trustworthiness. See also PREUSED.

**Writs fly** I do not know what started it but for the last half-dozen
years or so it has been almost obligatory in the press and on
radio (and hence in ordinary speech) always to describe writs
and summonses as airborne. ('Mention Maxwell and the writs are
sure to fly...'). This, however, applies only to actions for libel or
defamation. The Holy Writ certainly never flew, though
injunctions (which are merely another kind of writ) may also
sometimes take off.

# Y

**Yak-Yak** (or Yakity Yak) A derisive description of someone
talking incessantly or too much; often accompanied by a
movement of the fingers against the thumb, opening and closing
as if mimicking the action of a person's jaws.

**Yellowhat** See HARDHAT.

**Ye olde...** Cliché prefix describing anything self-consciously
old-fashioned, quaintly antique or purposely 'antiqued', like 'Ye
Olde Englysshe Tea Shoppe'. In such bogus applications this
would be pronounced 'Ye old-ee English-ee Tea Shop-ee',

whereas in genuine archaic (i.e. non-standardised, free) spelling a final e would have been almost soundless up to the late middle ages and completely so afterwards. And the initial Y of 'Ye' is merely a modern typographical or calligraphic substitute for the 'thorn', an old symbol for the English 'th' sound.

**Yesterday's men**   To the uninvolved bystander the hazards that lurk in the coining of political SLOGANS are a constant delight. After the Conservatives issued a poster depicting a queue of professional models pretending to be unemployed Britons, with the caption 'Labour isn't working', unemployment rose to record levels under the Tories. In May 1970 the Labour Party issued posters depicting caricatured Conservative leaders, with the slogan 'Yesterday's Men'. Little more than a year later, BBC television showed a programme of Labour leaders, by then in opposition, with the not inaccurate title *Yesterday's Men*, and there was outrage in the Labour ranks, resulting in a hostility to the BBC whose effect is still felt. (In 1978, incidentally, there appeared the illiterate Labour slogan 'Less Jobs, Less Houses, Less Hospitals – the Tories couldn't care less', which invited predictable comments and annotations about Less Grammar and Less Education under Labour).

**Yomping**   This word came into prominence during the Falklands War of 1982 and means laborious and energetic marching or tramping over considerable distances while carrying heavy knapsacks, or arms and ammunition, etc. The origin is unknown, but the Royal Marines are credited with its invention. The OED says that correspondents have linked the word to 'yumping', which is apparently something done by motorcar rally-drivers, but I would counter that with the old English injunction, TELL THAT TO THE MARINES. The fact that 'yomping' was on many lips and that everyone almost immediately knew its meaning is a tribute to the MEDIA: previous wars, fought without the benefit of television, impressed their coinages far more slowly and gradually on the public's imagination. However, like FRATTING with German women in the years immediately following the Second World War, yomping looks like being a soon-to-be-forgotten word, in spite of attempts by facetious journalists to use it figuratively (e.g. 'Mrs Thatcher may begin yomping round the hustings considerably sooner...' – *The Listener*).

**You know something?** Conversational opener and a declaration of interestedness meaning 'I'm going to say something to you'; and requiring no reply. The phrase is American, but was originally a direct translation from the German '*Weißt Du was?*'

**You name it** Colloquial equivalent of 'etc', used when a speaker (often a person being interviewed) has run out of examples or of things to say. From the commercial catch-phrase, 'You name it – we have it'.

**Young fogeys** See FOGEY.

**Your guess is as good as mine** Seven-word equivalent of 'I don't know'.

**You've read the book...** Advertising cliché used when books are made into plays or films – but one that was effectively ruined when, after *Watership Down* (an unlikely tale about clever talking rabbits) was made into a film, a butcher earned nationwide applause for a shop-window notice: 'You've read the book, you've seen the film – now try the pie'.

**Yuck** Expression of mock disgust at the taste or quality of whatever is so described. Onomatopoeic, from the noise of retching, or imminent vomiting. The adjective is yucky. But see below.

**Yummies** See YUPPIES.

**Yummy** Food manufacturers', television cooks' and food or cookery writers' pseudo-juvenile-twee advertising jargon-word describing the allegedly appetising quality of a dish or product. Copied from children's lip-smacking noises. The opposite of 'yummie' is YUCKY, above. Yummy-lovers are generally female, but no-one should under-rate the facetiousness of some television cooks who sail in the lee of the 'Galloping Gourmet', once celebrated for his embarrassing bouts of logorrhoea. One such culinary entertainer now follows in the G.G.'s wake by always having a glass of wine handy from which he takes the occasional 'slurpette', as he calls it, while preparing his yummy dishes.

**Yuppies** Near-acronym for 'Young Urban Professional Persons',
but also often explained as 'Young Upwardly Mobile Professional
Persons', usually those able to earn ASTRONOMICAL salaries,
disproportionate to the effort expended, in money markets; and
some, no doubt, who owe their upward mobility to INSIDER DEALING
in the CITY. ('Yumpies' would perhaps be more accurate for the
second explanation, but acronym-makers bend the rules.) Several
people have laid claim to the coining of the word, but it seems to
be generally agreed that it comes from the American financial
markets. And journalists have, of course, exploited the craze to
the full with facetious 'yuppie' coinages being added almost daily,
like 'yummies', who are not FOODIES but Young Upwardly Mobile
Marxists. The fad will eventually work itself out through OVERKILL.
Meanwhile, see also DINKIES, FOGEYS and SLOANE RANGERS.

# COLOUR SUPPLEMENT

**Black** 'A word of difficult history' say the original editors of the
OED. But the etymological difficulties they encountered around
1930 are as nothing compared to the troubles the word has run
into in the last decade; and they would have been astonished by
the demands that were to be made some four or five decades
later for changes in usage. For the OED defines black as 'dark,
sombre, dusky, gloomy, deeply stained with dirt; soiled, dirty,
foul, having dark or deadly purposes; malignant, pertaining to
or involving death; deadly, baneful, disastrous, sinister,
iniquitous, atrocious, horribly wicked; clouded with sorrow or
melancholy, dismal, gloomy, sad, threatening, boding ill; the
opposite of bright and hopeful, indicating disgrace, censure,
liability to punishment; having the face made dark crimson or
purple by strangulation, passion, or strenuous or violent effort;
discoloured by beating, bruising or pinching (of the human body);
to stain, sully, defame . . .' And so it goes on for page after page –
some 130 inches in small type, from funerals and mourning to
deadly snakes and spiders, the Black Death, Black Fridays, Black
Sheep of the family, the Black Hole of Calcutta; Blackguards giving
each other Black Looks, or getting into Black Books, hanging
judges donning their Black Cap; people squeezing their
Blackheads and hundreds of other 'black' expressions daily used
by persons who would never dream of saying an unkind word to
or about a non-European. In the British trades union movement
strike-breakers have always been reviled as Blacklegs (Blackleg
is a disease suffered by sheep, and when animals are sick they
are shunned by their fellows, though 'scab' is gaining ground as
being a more suitable insult to scream on the on picket-lines).
Members of gentlemen's clubs dread being Blackballed or
Blackmailed, for it would be a Black Mark against their character,
and witches dabble in the Black Arts. During the Second World
War there was the Black Market, when abnormal conditions of
supply-and-demand were exploited by racketeers who dealt
lucratively in goods that were rationed or otherwise in short

supply; and now there is the Black Economy. It was against this background of ancient usage that the Negro human-rights activist, the Rev. Martin Luther King, in 1967 launched a poster campaign with the slogan 'Black is Beautiful' (and incidentally also gave rise to such terms as 'Black CONSCIOUSNESS' and 'racial AWARENESS'). 'Black' had been until then – and not surprisingly in view of the foregoing – considered an insulting description when applied to a Negro person, especially as the skin colour of most Afro-Caribbeans is not a true black but comes in various shades of brown. Before King the polite, factual word was Negro (from Latin *niger*, Hispanic *negro*), though never 'nigger', which was and remains offensive. (Nigger brown, incidentally, was a standard shade in the colour-charts until the word was recognised as offensive: it is now changed to 'Scorched Earth'!) King in effect declared official the defiant use of 'black' and by implication decreed that 'Negro' that would henceforth be derogatory. It was almost as if the Jews had decided that they wanted no longer to be called Jews, would, moreover, consider it an insult, and made it known that they now took a pride in being 'Yids'. Unfortunately usage can not be suddenly changed in such a wilful way, even with a poster campaign and a vociferous protest movement behind it. And so the English language is now stuck with hundreds of ancient, respectable expressions which black people understandably find offensive. Various groups like trades unions and other bodies courageously try to speed benevolent linguistic change by 'blacking' old union expressions like 'blacking' or 'blacklegging' by (as the National Union of Journalists has nobly but vainly laid down in its rules) – 'substituting wherever possible other terms such as boycotting' – thus offending instead Captain Boycott and his fellow-Irishmen and generally making asses of themselves. LOONY local authorities, especially but not exclusively in London, have embarked on a deblacking process with a zeal comparable to the Nazis' attempts to burn all books by Jewish authors. To some extent the process is self-regulating as the language naturally finds its own levels. For example, one seldom now hears the area round Birmingham and Wolverhampton described as the Black Country, partly because so much of the old smoke-creating industries have disappeared, and partly because large areas of the Midlands have high concentrations of ETHNIC people from the Indian subcontinent. But the pursuit of allegedly racist usages is relentless, bringing ridicule even on the well-meaning. A London school-teacher, for example, wrote to the parents of a 5-year-old mentally handicapped child who had painfully managed to learn a nursery-rhyme and recited it at school: 'We do not encourage the rhyme "Baa Baa Black Sheep" because it has been identified as racially derogatory and is actively discouraged by Islington council.' Another London council has ordered the words to be changed to 'Baa Baa Green Sheep'. Such zeal, incidentally, is not shared by American Blacks and rights workers, who have yet to insist on a name-change for the White House in Washington. Nor by African governments, which continue to erect 'Accident Black Spot' warning-signs on the countries' roads.

**Blue** The colour of depression, murder, harlots and the modern British Conservative Party. The Tories' use of the colour dates from only comparatively recent times – see under RED below. Blue is also the colour of fear and cowardice (a blue funk) or lewdness (blue films or movies) and of certain occasional parliamentary publications bound in blue covers and since the early 18th century called Blue Books (see also WHITE PAPERS, below). The British police are affectionately known as The Boys in Blue, and less affectionately, in the past, since Shakespeare, as Bluebottles (who appear when one screams Blue Murder?); and their ranks, when stretched, traditionally known as The Thin Blue Line (an adaptation from The Thin Red Line, the 93rd Foot Regiment in the Crimean War). Many police-stations in Britain have a blue lamp outside, and police-cars flashing ones, as do other emergency vehicles. In the Second World War the official censor wielded a blue pencil in the letters-home of soldiers who might have revealed too much information, hence to Blue-pencil something that is censored. In those days the word 'bloody' was considered near-blasphemous (allegedly but unconvincingly an abbreviated form of 'by our Lady') and was often removed from comedy scripts with bold strokes of the censor's blue pencil. Hence 'bluepencilled' also became a euphemism for bloody, because both words shared the first two letters: 'I was feeling bluepencilled awful', before 'bloody' turned into an everyday word. It was long believed by some that aristocratic people had bluer blood in their veins than commoners, hence 'blue-blooded'. Since the 18th century intellectual women have laboured under the description 'Bluestockings'. In the Catholic

religion the garments of the Virgin Mary are traditionally
coloured blue, as a symbol of fidelity. But blue was also the
prescribed 'dress of ignominy for a harlot in the house of
correction' (OED). In the Jewish tradition, pale blue is the colour
of prudence and goodness, and has been adopted for the pale-
blue-and-white flag of the state of Israel, probably in order to
heed the injunction of the Old Testament (Numbers IX 38): 'Speak
unto the children of Israel, and bid them that they make them
fringes on the border of their garments . . . a ribband of blue.'
Bluebeards are wife-murderers, even to journalists who have
never read Perrault's *Tales* of 1697 in which he first figures;
Bluejackets are sailors. The Blues are a form of American negro
singing which express their people's sadness (and usually begin
'I woke up dis morning. . .'). But 'feeling blue', or 'having a fit of
the blues', or 'the blue devils' are names for anything from a fit
of mild depression to *delirium tremens*. Blueprints are architects'
or engineers' plans printed by a diazo method of reproduction,
now superseded by other forms of reprography; but the word is
still a favourite in the press as a cliché description for future plans.
A Blue Funk for extreme fear was popularised, if not invented, by
Thomas Hughes in *Tom Brown's Schooldays* (1857), and touch-
papers for lighting and firing explosive charges by the British
Army were traditionally blue – perhaps for use in the BROWN Bess,
below.

**Brown** The colour of excreta, Wagner and the Nazis. It was this
composer's favourite colour, and as Adolf Hitler admired him
and his theories on race and Teutonic superiority (which he
adopted and murderously improved upon) he chose this colour
for the uniforms of the *Sturmabteilung*, the SA Brownshirts. As the
Americans had a White House, Hitler naturally called his party
headquarters the Brown House (perhaps the earliest 'dirty
protest'!); and he also had his manifestos and Nazi books printed
in brown ink. In English brown, also dun(g), is not a favourite
colour to talk picturesquely about, apart from being 'in a brown
study' ('a state of mental abstraction or musings, or gloomy
meditations'). Apples, turnips, etc. which suffer from internal
decay are said to have a disease called Brownheart. Bored British
soldiers before and during the Second World War declared that
they were Browned Off – perhaps when they felt BLUE. They
affectionately called a certain kind of rifle Brown Bess, because

of its polished, nut-brown stock – a practice going back to the early 18th century (strange how many lethal weapons were given women's names!). In the 1930s and 40s the boxer Joe Louis was known as the Brown Bomber, because he was black. (Today a Black Bomber is one of many names of a certain illicit narcotic.) 'Blacks' (see above) in fact are nearly always of an attractive brown skin colour, and many Britons who show an irrational colour prejudice against immigrants take the first available opportunity to make their own faces and bodies as brown as possible, returning from holidays or the sun-bed parlour darker than many a Tamil. Brown bread was formerly considered an undesirable kind of cheap, rough staple food made for the poor from unrefined flour, but the WHOLE food movement has now reversed this trend; although Caxton liked it in the late 1400s: 'Bryng me som broun brede and water in a treen dyshe.' The same goes for Brown Rice, formerly cheaper because it was unpolished, now desired by health-food FANS for the beneficial coarseness of its roughage. Even Gravy Browning, that old standby of the lazy cook, which imparts an uninviting brown colour to soups and sauces, has a pejorative ring, at least to those who care about good food; and every Briton remembers with distaste from his schooldays having to eat Brown Windsor Soup (not to be confused with Brown Windsor Soap). In Britain Junior Girl Scouts are innocently called Brownies, though not elsewhere, especially not in the United States, where brownie stands for something extremely unpleasant in the amatory vocabulary of homosexuals. Also from the United States is the insulting nickname Brown-nose for a sycophant, explained in Webster's Dictionary (1961) 'from the implication that servility is tantamount to having one's nose in the anus of the person from whom advancement is sought'. The British parliament publishes Blue, White or Green Papers (see above and below) but no Brown Paper, though when Jack and Jill met with their accident it provided a useful plaster, steeped in vinegar.

**Gold** seldom is, even when it glitters, glisters or glittereth, but the word is usually used for exaggeration or hyperbole. In printing, gold is really yellow ink containing metallic fragments; golden human hair means blond; and in cooking ('fry till golden'), it comes in various shades of light brown.

**Green** is the colour of verdure, freshness and innocence, perhaps as enjoyed by someone in his Salad Days; also, to some extent, and as a faint insult, the colour of simplemindedness. It is also now the name of ecological political parties in several countries. They were at first merely nicknamed 'The Greens' but later adopted the colour and name officially. Green would also be suitable for political parties which believe in making the rich poor and the poor poorer, i.e. green with envy, though both Labour and communists and other revolutionary movements have always favoured RED. There is also an old English euphemism 'giving a girl a green gown', meaning having sexual intercourse with her. This comes from the fact that in rural England and before the advent of the motor-car, illicit love-making was largely an outdoor pastime; and grass has a tiresome way of leaving its marks on clothing. The Elizabethan tune 'My Lady Greensleeves' means nothing more nor less than that the lady was willing. There is no male equivalent, but if there were it would presumably be 'My Lord Green-knees', or 'Green-elbows'. In institutional kitchens and dining-rooms, e.g. schools and hospitals, where bad food is a hallowed British tradition, allegedly health-giving Greens are vegetables that have had all the goodness and most of their colour boiled out of them. In the language of JOURNOS 'getting (or giving) the green light' means to obtain (or give) approval for something – from the colour sequence of traffic lights on both road and rail; although the RED light is a different analogy altogether. Irish patriots go MAUDLIN or misty-eyed when they hear 'The Wearing of the Green', for that is the national colour of the Emerald Isle; and property-developers cast a different sort of envious eye on the Green Belt, which is supposed to be free from their depredations. Gifted gardeners are said to have Green Fingers (though they are usually ingrained with earth) and pale, adolescent girls used to suffer from the romantic-sounding Green Sickness – for which there is now doubtless a more down-to-earth name. Government Green Papers are consultative documents without force of law.

**Grey** is the indeterminate colour – some say not a real colour but a shade, a mixture of different amounts of black and white with additions of other pigments, making it pinky-grey, green-grey, blue-grey, etc. Hence perhaps the undefinable Grey Areas. To possess plenty of Grey Matter, however, is a POSITIVE quality, for it is what the active part of the brain consists of: a scientific fact, as the stuff really is grey, though calling it grey matter is described as 'pseudo-scientific' by those authorities who prefer to cloak their medical terms in the decent obscurity of Latin. An influential elder person who wields indirect power while keeping what would now be called a low profile, is a Grey Eminence, uneasily translated from the French, where it referred to the undue political influence of a specific cleric. Because human hair goes white with age, the mixture of the two producing shades of grey, it is also (apart from whatever Grey Matter is possessed) the colour of implied wisdom. In other applications 'pepper-and-salt' would do. After Blacks in America advocated racial violence by forming the Black Panthers, there appeared a group of old persons purporting to fight, equally militantly, for the rights of the aged (see 'Forward') calling themselves the Grey Panthers. But 'in the dark,' according to the proverb, 'all cats are grey'.

**Orange**  The orange, say the reference-books, is 'a large globose many-celled berry with sub-acid juicy pulp, enclosed in a tough rind of a bright reddish-yellow ( = orange) colour'. It is the symbol of comparatively little: chiefly Ulster Protestants and marriage – including the union of the Liberals and the Social Democrats. The fruit was originally called 'a norange', from Hispanic, Persian and Arab words like *naranja, naranj, narang*, etc, but the *n*, as every schoolboy knows, was transferred to the indefinite article for the sake of elision and euphony. If that pretty story is true it happened a long time ago, as the OED has a 13th-century instance of an *orenge*. The colour is unusual in possessing, on the whole, only good associations, though some may have reservations about a few over-vociferous Orangemen from the MILITANT Ulster Protestants. They owe their political colour to an accident. There is, on the River Rhone in France, a town called Orange which has absolutely nothing to do with the fruit but which in 1530 passed into the hands of the House of Nassau, later the royal rulers of Holland. The Protestant William III, remembering the name of his conquest, adopted the – quite unconnected – orange as his symbol and its colour for his flags, cockades and other appurtenances of his House of Orange. After the revolution of 1689 and the Battle of the Boyne of 1690, in which William III defeated James II and his French allies, Ulster Protestants, now Orangemen, never looked back. Orange has at different times been the colour of the Liberal

Party (Blue, Green and Yellow were also used at times) and latterly that of the Liberal/SDP alliance, though this has never been used with the devotion of the Tories' true-blue and the SOCIALISTS' blood-red and latterly true-pink (see below). Orange-blossom as a decoration carried by brides in WHITE weddings became fashionable in France in the early years of the 19th century: 'Women at their marriage wear a crown of orange buds and blossoms; hence the orange-blossom is taken as a symbol of marriage.'

**Pink** The colour both of femininity and effeminacy; also of good health ('in the pink'). From the early 17th to the early 19th century 'a Pin(c)k(e)' was a pretty girl. *The Sporting Pink* was printed on pink paper, and some sporting papers, notably the football edition of *The Liverpool Echo*, still are. Foxhunting men and women wear scarlet coats but paradoxically always refer to them as being Pink – perhaps in order to catch out the socially-unspeakable who know nothing about chasing the fox. *Pink* is the Dutch word for the little finger, hence the American name for it, pinky. A Pinky-crooker is an over-genteel person – one who affectedly crooks his little finger when holding a cup, knife or fork. American negroes (though presumably not Black Panthers) approvingly call a pretty and light-skinned negro girl a Pinky or Pink-toes; and indeed American BLACKS generally call 'whites' Pinks, perhaps derisively and in retaliation but certainly more accurately than calling them whites, just as they themselves are seldom if ever really black. Pinko was once a synonym of blotto, i.e. very drunk – a state in which one is said to see imaginary pink elephants – and after which one doubtless needs to empty one's bladder, or have a Pinkle. Partridge says this association with liquids may have been a reference to pink blotting-paper and its qualities of soaking-up spillages. Today's Pinkoes are communists, or at any rate FELLOW TRAVELLERS who claim not to be members of the party (i.e. REDS) but clearly sympathise with its aims. In 1986 the Labour Party officially ditched the red flag (the actual symbolical flag, not the tune – see below) and invited its followers to march behind a new emblem, the Pink Rose. They must have been unaware that this was already the trade-mark of Mills and Boon, publishers of love stories and romances. Or perhaps they were saying that many of their idealistic policies were based on romantic fiction.

**Purple**  The colour of royalty, justice, the law and authority.
Purple passages in novels, however, are in over-heated prose
with luridly romantic undertones. Football commentators speak
of teams 'going through a purple patch' when they are thought
to be playing with energy and conviction. American soldiers, etc.
are awarded the Purple Heart medal, their equivalent of the
British Victoria Cross, but the name was later somewhat devalued
as more and more of them took to the other Purple Hearts, a
nickname for amphetamine-based illicit stimulant drugs.


**Red**  as the colour of socialism arose from the spilling of blood. It
was the French who gruesomely started the trend – not in 1789
(when the red flag was used only because it had been the ancient
Roman Empire signal calling men to arms) but in the bloodier,
more widespread, 1848 revolution. In this, *les républicains rouges*
had the less than engaging habit of dipping their hands in the
gore of their victims to brandish during triumphal processions,
rather as Arab FUNDAMENTALISTS still do to this day (though they
also use their own, and each others' blood for this purpose). From
then on, red was firmly established as the colour of republicanism
and revolt, but by no means universally so. Although *Punch* in
1851 already parodied the hit tune from Balfe's *Bohemian Girl* as
'I dreamt that I stood in Crystal halls/With Chartists and Reds at
my side . . .' there was published as late as 1907 *True Red*,
described as 'The Magazine of Wirral Conservatives' (See BLUE).
And when Henry Mond stood as a Tory in the East Toxteth
parliamentary by-election in 1929, his election address ('Socialism
kills individuality . . . Liberal unity is a myth . . .') was printed in a
bright, socialist red – perhaps presciently, as the Monds later
turned into the Labour Lords Melchett. Red is still the favourite
colour of hotheaded revolutionaries – of the infamous Chinese
Red Guards, the European Red Brigades and Red Army Faction –
the last-named abbreviated to RAF, which is a monstrous affront
to those who died in the Royal Air Force for the cause of freedom.
The Red Flag is still the British Labour Party's official anthem, a
lugubrious dirge adapted from a German Christmas carol, *O
Tannenbaum, O Tannenbaum/Wie grün sind deine Blätter!* –
which extols the everlasting GREEN of the fir-tree. An early English
translation of this carol begins, 'O hemlock-tree, O hemlock-
tree/How bitter are thy branches!'

**White** Much to the disgust of those who – very properly –
campaign for racial equality-of-opportunity, white is the ancient
colour signifying purity, truth, goodness, hope and innocence,
for it is the colour of newly-washed linen on which unclean stains
would show, whereas dark colours may hide the dirt. After the
resurrection, Jesus was traditionally depicted wearing white, and
it is also one of the Pope's three colours (in addition to RED and
PURPLE, but white appears to be what football-supporters would
describe as his 'away-colour'). In the First World War men who
failed to volunteer for military service were often sent white
feathers denoting cowardice (but see below), probably because
a white bird used to be the symbol of man's conscience. However,
some sources claim it comes from cock-fighting, in which birds
with white tail-feathers were thought to be of inferior fighting
stock. White-collar workers are those who work in offices, etc.
and have to dress formally (the hyphen is important but usually
neglected, making nonsense of the term), derived from the now
happily defunct habit of men wearing the same shirt for a week,
changing only the parts that showed the dirt, namely the –
separately attached – collar and cuffs. A White Flag is the signal
for surrender (do all armies carry one, just in case?); a White Lie,
one which is designed to spare the recipient's feelings; a White
Night, said by some to be a sleepless one, though others say it
means the opposite, i.e. a night spent with a woman but abstaining
from sex and therefore presumably sleeping (clearly not with a
White Slave, the purpose of whose bondage is sexual
prostitution). The British government issues White Papers, which
are documents intended to inform Parliament of whatever is
discussed in them but are also available to the public via Her
Majesty's Stationery Office (see also BLUE papers). The
appearance of reformatory proposals in such a publication may
be attended by much pious noise but that, in effect, is usually the
end of it. ('They draw up resolutions, issue a report – and let the
matter drop . . .', said a parliamentary wit, '. . . after which they
use a great deal of White Paper . . .'). Because white is also the
symbol of virginity and purity, most girls prefer a White
Wedding – which if statistics are to be believed would make white
the colour of a joke, as most western brides relinquish their
purity before marriage. This brings me to a Whited Sepulchre,
from *St Matthew* XXIII, 27, in which Jesus is reported as saying
'Ye are like unto whited sepulchres, which indeed appear

beautiful outwards but are within full of dead men's bones, and full of all uncleanness'. Persons accused (rightly or wrongly) of political crimes in totalitarian regimes can afterwards be rehabilitated or WHITEWASHED. A white elephant is an unwanted or useless possession: because, says *Brewer's Dictionary of Phrase and Fable*, a King of Siam was once in the habit of presenting a white elephant to any courtier he wished to ruin – a sort of extremely heavy hint.

**Yellow**  The colour of fear, jealousy, treachery and cowardice, of saffron, egg-yolks, lemons, primroses, sulphur, jaundice and canaries. The French used to daub yellow marks on the doors of men accused of cowardice, and for many centuries since the middle ages (and again under the Nazis) Jews were obliged to wear yellow patches or stars, probably derived from the fact that in ancient religious art Judas is often depicted wearing that colour. The murderous behaviour of the JAPS (then known as 'Yellow Bastards') during the Second World War did little to enhance the reputation of the colour, although the friendly Chinese used to be equally inaccurately described as being of yellow skin-colour. Ever since the Far East was opened to western influences and China and Japan began to follow western nations by industrialisation and rising militarism, their threat has been described as the Yellow Peril. The Yellow Press, however, is the all-American name for the – alas no longer all-American – sensationalising, truth-distorting, headline-grabbing, silly-punning gutter press (also known as TABLOIDS).